Amy G. Oden

Foreword by Marjorie J. Thompson

Right Here Right Now

The Practice *of* Christian Mindfulness

Abingdon Press
Nashville

RIGHT HERE RIGHT NOW:
THE PRACTICE OF CHRISTIAN MINDFULNESS

Copyright © 2017 by Abingdon Press

All rights reserved.

No part of this work may be reproduced or transmitted in any form or by any means, electronic or mechanical, including photocopying and recording, or by any information storage or retrieval system, except as may be expressly permitted by the 1976 Copyright Act or in writing from the publisher. Requests for permission can be addressed to Permissions, The United Methodist Publishing House, 2222 Rosa L. Parks Blvd., PO Box 280988, Nashville, TN, 37228-0988 or e-mailed to permissions@abingdonpress.com.

Library of Congress Cataloging-in-Publication Data has been requested.

ISBN 978-1-5018-3249-9

Unless otherwise indicated, all Scripture quotations are from the Common English Bible. Copyright © 2011 by the Common English Bible. All rights reserved. Used by permission. www.CommonEnglishBible.com.

Scripture quotations marked (KJV) are taken from The Authorized (King James) Version. Rights in the Authorized Version in the United Kingdom are vested in the Crown. Reproduced by permission of the Crown's patentee, Cambridge University Press.

Scripture quotations marked (The Message) are taken from *THE MESSAGE.* Copyright © by Eugene H. Peterson 1993, 1994, 1995, 1996, 2000, 2001, 2002. Used by permission of NavPress Publishing Group.

Scripture quotations marked (NRSV) are taken from the New Revised Standard Version of the Bible, copyright 1989, Division of Christian Education of the National Council of the Churches of Christ in the United States of America. Used by permission. All rights reserved.

Scripture quotations marked (NIV) are taken from the Holy Bible, New International Version®, NIV®. Copyright © 1973, 1978, 1984, 2011 by Biblica, Inc.™ Used by permission of Zondervan. All rights reserved worldwide. www.zondervan.com. The "NIV" and "New International Version" are trademarks registered in the United States Patent and Trademark Office by Biblica, Inc.™

17 18 19 20 21 22 23 24 25—10 9 8 7 6 5 4 3 2 1

MANUFACTURED IN THE UNITED STATES OF AMERICA

For Walker

. . . .

Contents

Contents

Foreword

Back in the 1990s, a series of books featuring "magic eyes" became popular. Each page of these books presented a colorful mass of indecipherable squiggles and abstract patterns that appeared to be randomly designed. But if you gazed on the image with "soft eyes"—allowing your vision to become slightly blurred and unfocused—an intriguing three-dimensional image would slowly emerge from the two-dimensional surface of the page. A clear and often stunningly intricate image was embedded in what first appeared to be an abstract design. When you got the hang of seeing this way, you could consciously move back and forth between your ordinary perception of each page and the figures hidden within its 2-D surface.

Reading Amy Oden's book *Right Here Right Now: The Practice of Christian Mindfulness* brought to mind my experience of seeing with "magic eyes." From the surface jumble of a distracted and distracting culture, from the sometimes confusing diversity of spiritual traditions in our globally connected world, from the variety of spiritual practices and understandings within Christian scripture and history, Amy opens our eyes to an emerging central image. She deftly lifts up a clear template for what lies at the core of all spiritual practice: mindfulness—a simple awareness within ordinary life of divine presence, here and now. "Christian mindfulness is the practice of paying prayerful attention in the present moment to God's abundant life," she writes. For those of us familiar with Brother Lawrence's counsel to "practice the presence of God" in all things, even the most mundane, Oden's definition of mindfulness will sound like a fresh angle on the great tradition of Christian contemplation. Not surprisingly, our author does not neglect Brother Lawrence in her overview of Christian saints and mystics who have championed continual awareness of divine presence!

Amy hopes this book may offer a way for Christians to engage more hospitably with people of other faiths or with no faith. Yet her first concern is to help Christians see that while the term may not be found in our scriptures, the essence of mindfulness is deeply embedded in classic Judeo-Christian spiritual teaching and practice. Pointing out that God is always mindful of us (Ps 8:4), the author shows how the biblical invitation for humans to reciprocate in mindfulness of God is expressed in various ways: remembrance of divine constancy; staying awake, or alert to what is really happening; listening deeply— "having eyes to see and ears to hear," as Jesus repeatedly puts it.

Beyond rooting the essence of mindfulness in Hebrew and Christian tradition, Oden takes care to distinguish from a biblical perspective what is distinctively Christian about this practice. "Christian mindfulness is a way to abide in Christ," she observes. Unlike many generic practices of mindfulness now popular in business, education, and the fitness industry, the author underscores that Christian mindfulness is not an end in itself but an awareness that turns us toward God: "The goal of Christian mindfulness is … an experience of our lives in God, our true home." Christian mindfulness leads not only to greater physical and mental well-being but clearer discernment of divine activity and guidance, both personally and collectively. Indeed, Oden urges, one of the significant responsibilities of Christians engaged in mindfulness is "curating" the practice— clarifying, interpreting, sifting from its cultural manifestations that which genuinely reflects Christlikeness. She identifies five key marks of the "renewal of our minds" in Christ: freedom, authenticity, root-edness, gratitude, and open-hearted compassion.

Written in an engaging modern idiom without theological jar-gon, Amy addresses contemporary issues that will appeal to multiple generations. She speaks to mindfulness in online communication through texting, e-mail, and social media. Importantly, technology is not identified as the enemy but rather our mind's way of absorbing and reacting to it. Mindfulness helps to free us from reactivity and fear, an especially timely practice in today's highly polarized socio-political climate. Oden's segment on mindful social action is also deeply relevant for our day. As we become more awake to ways we participate in unjust systems, and more aware of where God is counteracting our personal and collective destructiveness, we are re-minded of who is redeeming this world. Only then can we partici-pate with God in the healing of the world and our own hearts.

This book is eminently practical. Regular prompts to reflection and practice punctuate the writing. Amy's introduction to mindful practice is a simple four-step process, easy to understand and follow. The real treasure of this book will come through putting the four steps into habitual practice in daily life, and Oden gives us plenty of avenues for doing so. As the author points out, the book is characterized by a certain level of thematic repetition. She suggests that her readers ap-ply mindful observation to their experience of this aspect of the book. I might further suggest that we allow the repeated ideas to sink into our hearts like the repeated elements of worship liturgy, or the way repeated phrases of scripture can "build themselves a little nest in our hearts"—to borrow a phrase from my early mentor, Henri Nouwen.

If we can let Amy's words become a litany of invitation into the posture of open-hearted presence to the Presence, right here, right now, I feel confident that the fruit of the Spirit—and of this book—will come to mark our lives and delight our Maker!

—Marjorie J. Thompson, Pentecost, 2017

Introduction

What Is This Book About?

C hristian mindfulness practice is rooted in the most basic witness of Jesus: God with us, right here, right now. Jesus proclaims, The reign of God is at hand! here, now available for all, *if* we pay attention. Or, as Jesus says, if we have eyes to see and ears to hear. If we are mindful. To live out the reign of God requires mindful lives, intentionally aware in each present moment of God's life and mission in the world. Christian mindfulness, then, is an anchoring practice, a way to abide in Christ.

My purpose in this book is to clarify and trace the roots of Christian mindfulness and offer some starting points for its practice today. My hope is that this book will help Christians, especially leaders, understand its roots and possibilities as a Christian practice. Moreover, as a fundamental Christian witness to the good news, Christian mindfulness practice can

- draw Christian communities more deeply into God's presence with us;

- hold us accountable to God's mission in the world beyond our institutions and churches; and

- offer a relevant point for Christians to hospitably engage the world and people of other faiths and no faith, aware of the genuinely different vocabularies and understandings of mindfulness around us.

The structure of the book is as follows: Chapter 1 offers a working definition for Christian mindfulness and lays out both the distinctives and marks of Christian mindfulness. Chapter 2 identifies roots of mindfulness both in Christian tradition and current culture as Christians are called upon to curate these resources for faithful witness in the world. Chapter 3 details many methods for mindfulness practice today both for individuals and communities. Chapter 4 turns to the difference that Christian mindfulness practice can make for Christian witness in the world today. Sidebar questions throughout invite you to engage mindfully as you read.

This project on Christian mindfulness is born out of my vocation to invite ancient mothers and fathers in the faith to bear witness for Christian life and witness in the world today. My hunch is that if Macrina or Benedict were observing popular mindfulness practices today, they would have some wisdom regarding its particular expressions among those who follow Jesus. Several observations of my own prompt me to explore the conversation between historical Christian witness and the current mindfulness movement. The first observation is that mindfulness practices have gained widespread popularity across many different sectors of American society. The second observation is that many Christians are practicing mindfulness at yoga class or at work seemingly unaware of its roots in Christian prayer or actively concerned that their practice may be incompatible with Christian faith. Third, there are many Christians who denounce all mindfulness practice out of hand, either because they believe it is strictly Buddhist, or because they believe it is not Christian. My fourth observation is that many nonreligious practitioners of mindfulness are also unaware of its roots in the Christian tradition and might be surprised, or even troubled, to discover family resemblances between their own practice and its expression in Christianity. Lastly, many Christian leaders and pastors are uninformed or ill equipped to help Christians locate mindfulness practice within Christian faith and tradition. Because of this, many leaders are confused about how to engage this pervasive practice faithfully. Indeed, there is an embarrassment of riches when it comes to mindfulness practice across many cultures and faiths, each with its own history and practice. This book is intended not to privilege Christian mindfulness above these other forms, but rather to clarify and trace its roots as a Christian spiritual practice.

Why Now?

Another book on spirituality? Really? When there is so much suffering in the world?

I take this question seriously because it's one I continually ask. Perhaps especially when there is so much suffering in the world we are better able to see it and to act with compassion and justice when we are spiritually rooted than when we are blown by winds of reactivity. Superficial Christian responses to suffering too often do harm while blinding us with the conviction that we are "helping." This question also reveals a corrosive dualism that continues to plague Christianity, opposing "spirituality" to "social justice," "people who pray" versus "people who act." The deep spiritual lives of some of the greatest Christian social activists of late modernity, such as Dorothy Day, Martin Luther King Jr., and Dietrich Bonhoeffer, witness to the necessary integration of prayer and action.

Confusion about this within some Christian circles has led to unnecessary suspicion and even division between those focused on social justice and those focused on Christian spiritual formation.

About Words

There are several phrases I use throughout this book that each carry their own inescapable linguistic baggage. The first is language for God. The hubris of trying to say anything at all about the One beyond human knowing is tempered by our longing to give witness to the glory of God in our midst, even within the fraught limits of language. As a Christian, I will use not only "God," "Jesus," and "Holy Spirit" but also other biblical names for God, such as "Lord," "Creator," "Source," and "One." Often, I will use "God's life" rather than simply "God" in order to convey the dynamic, lived reality of the Triune God with us here now.

The second is the phrase "kingdom of God." Jesus's proclamation of the good news of this kingdom at hand is the central witness of the Christian faith. It is a new heaven and new earth ordered by God's love, a reality both here now and also yet to come in its fullness. I use several expressions of the phrase, including "reign of God," "rule of God," "God's abundant life," "God's dream for the world," and "missio Dei," all intended to convey the dynamic, lived reality of God's ongoing mission to renew all creation.

The third is language about "the culture," "American culture," or "current culture." In a multicultural world there is no one "culture." Moreover, using the singular "culture" can serve to universalize dominant white culture, rendering invisible the rich tapestries of cultures that shape our lives. With this in mind, I have tried to use multiple phrasings, such as "cultural landscape," to convey the complex and fluid character of today's multicultural world. We should note that the ancient world was also multicultural, offering another relevant point of intersection with postmodernity.

The fourth is the phrase that titles the book, "right here, right now," much-used throughout the book. One reader of an early draft helpfully warned me against its overuse as tedious and annoying. Still, because this claim, that God is right here, right now, is pivotal to a Christian understanding of mindfulness, and, indeed, to the entire Christian witness, it shows up a lot. I try to vary it with "in the present," "in this moment," and "here, now." If you are a reader who also finds this phrase overused or tedious, I invite you to practice mindfulness as you read: when you come upon this phrase, "right here, right now," pause, breathe deeply, and exhale, attentive to God's presence with you. Embody mindfulness practice as you read this book.

Lastly, I use the first-person plural, "we" and "us," to locate myself within the Christian family broadly construed. I know that not all readers share this identity.

About Limits

As an introduction to Christian mindfulness, this book cannot say everything and that can be painful when there is so much to cover! While I attempt to trace the biblical and historical roots of Christian mindfulness and offer starting points for its practice today, I am also aware that, as an introduction, this book is neither detailed nor exhaustive. Moreover, it is intended for a wide readership, so I try to avoid theological jargon and do not assume advanced knowledge of Christian spiritual traditions. I hope that professors of spiritual formation will find this book makes a great introduction for their students and that it offers a refresher for colleagues less familiar with this very ancient Christian practice of responding to God. Those familiar with the literature will recognize overlaps with the scholarship of other, wise mentors who employ varying vocabularies for Christian prayer that promote mindfulness.

Thanksgivings

I am grateful to all the communities that surround and support my vocation. Saint Paul School of Theology granted me research leave to pursue this project. The 2015 Wesley Studies Summer Seminar at Asbury Theological Seminary helped me develop early questions and trajectories of investigation. Communities within the Academy for Spiritual Formation (Upper Room Ministries) have provided fertile conversation and reflection on Christian mindfulness and prayer. David Teel, my editor, has offered tireless enthusiasm for this project. Colleagues, friends, and family have engaged in conversation to help me think and write more carefully. Many read drafts along the way. I particularly want to thank Susan Ross, Suzanne Seaton, L. Roger Owens, Carol Cook Moore, Kathy Shook McCallie, Jeni Markham Clewell, Pat Hoerth, Janice Meese Sharp, Kathy Leithner, Ginger Howl, David Wiggs, Jeannie Himes, Katrina McBride, Jared White, Pat Luna, Curt Gruel, Bobbie Roe, Ted Campbell, Steve Martyn, Ruth Anne Reese, Christine Pohl, Johnny Sears, Rebecca Laird, JD Wall, Jeremy Smith, Rachel McClain, Jamila Belt Oden, Brian Yelch, Kevin Watson, and Priscilla Pope-Levison. Thanks to my husband, Perry Williams, who blesses each day with holy conversation.

—July 19, 2016, The Feast of Macrina

Chapter 1

Christian Mindfulness

The Hunger of Our Time and Christian Mindfulness

We know it well, the tendency in American culture to rush through daily life at a breathless pace from one thing to the next, as we jump mentally ahead to the next thing while doing this one. We reply to e-mails and update our calendars while sitting in a meeting at work. We multitask our way through the day and pull into the driveway with no memory of driving home. We are numbed by overstimulation and continually preoccupied. We are never truly present to the moment we're actually living.

The hunger I hear about over and over from my students, friends, and neighbors is a hunger to live the real life that I'm living right here, right now. Not the life that happened yesterday as I replay a conversation over and over in my head. Not the life that will happen tomorrow as I anticipate a crammed day. Not the edited life that I project online. This is a hunger to live deeply and truly, to know and inhabit our own lives, to be at home in our lives right now.

Often this hunger is expressed through weariness with chronically over-scheduled lives. I hear this especially from parents and families. They hunger for a life that runs deep, not just wide. They describe a life diffused across the surface of things yet never able to stop and savor it deeply. This hunger is expressed as a longing for focus in the midst of distractions or as a desire for rootedness that goes deep rather than lives in scattered fragments. Sometimes we simply long to be one person living one life, rather than feeling like we are several people living multiple lives.

Jesus proclaims the good news of that life we are hungry for. True life he calls "abundant life." "I came so that they could have life—indeed, so that they could live life to the fullest" (John 10:10b). Abundant life is the life God desires for all of us. A life that is real, not fake. A life that is true, not false. A life awake in the present moment, not stuck in the past or fixated on the future. A life that is whole, not fragmented. A life that is rooted, not scattered. A life that is connected to those we love, not disembodied in distraction. A life grounded by love, not anxiety or fear.

Mindfulness practice can be a doorway to the abundant life Jesus offers. Through the practice of mindfulness we can wake up from a stupor of busyness and overstimulation. By becoming present to the world in front of us—and inside of us—we become at home in our own lives. Through the practice of mindfulness, we cultivate eyes to see and ears to hear God's very life in which we live and move and have our being, right here, right now. Christian mindfulness is *the practice of paying prayerful attention in the present moment to God's abundant life.*[1]

Let's unpack the notion of "paying prayerful attention." Put simply, "paying attention" means the act of using our awareness on purpose. We intentionally turn our attention away from preoccupations that pull us out of our current experience and, instead, turn toward this present moment. Adding the word *prayerful*, however, qualifies how we pay attention.

The word *prayerful* does not refer here to formal prayers. Rather, "prayerful" is more an orientation than a set of words or a right ritual. If prayer is "being ourselves with God," prayerful attention indicates a willingness to be ourselves, unedited and unguarded.[2] "Prayerful" means being real, not a smiley-face version of ourselves. Paying prayerful attention means paying *real* attention, not just going through the motions.

Moreover, prayerful means nonjudgmental in the sense of being available and openhearted. A prayerful posture does not presume to already know what our paying attention will reveal. That means we cannot pre-judge or frontload what we will discover when we pay prayerful attention. Rather, we are more open to discovery than judgment, more to listening than speaking. Prayerful attention expects to discover something about what God is up to. Thus, prayerful attention is curious and unhurried.

Lastly, notice that our definition of Christian mindfulness points our attention to *God's abundant life*. Later in this chapter, we will address this particularly Christian understanding of the way mindfulness connects us to God.

It's no surprise the mindfulness movement has spread rapidly in our culture, from yoga classes to corporate training. When people are hungry, they go where the food is. Mindfulness practices feed this hunger. Among your family and friends, Christians and non-Christians, it's likely you know some who are practicing mindfulness at work, at school, or at exercise class.

We are not alone in our hunger for authentic, abundant life. People have always had this hunger, so mindfulness has been around for millennia. Yet many, Christians and non-Christians alike, assume that mindfulness belongs exclusively to Buddhism or other eastern religions. Indeed, most world religions offer some form of mindfulness practice.

From the very beginning, Christianity, too, practiced mindfulness. The Gospels are full of Jesus's teaching about the critical importance of mindfulness for those who want kingdom lives. Spiritual teachers throughout the history of the church have pointed to mindfulness as foundational for prayer and connecting to God. As twenty-first-century Christians, we have rich resources for Christian mindfulness.

Jesus and Gospel Mindfulness: What Does Jesus Say about Mindfulness?

Pause and pay attention to your own awareness right now. It's likely that you rely first on your eyes and ears to become aware of your immediate surroundings, then move on to your internal bodily sensations and perceptions. Sight and sound are primary tools of sensory awareness for most people. Seeing and hearing focuses our immediate awareness on this concrete moment. Seeing and hearing can pull us from our mental mixtape of past conversations or future tasks into what is happening right now.

Stop reading and pay attention to your own awareness right now. When you look up from

4

this book, what do you see? What do you hear? Notice what sensations you feel in your body. Take a moment to become aware.

Jesus starts here, too. Throughout his teaching, he invites us into awareness. Again and again he says, "Whoever has ears to listen should pay attention!" (Mark 4:9) and "Happy are your eyes because they see. Happy are your ears because they hear" (Matt 13:16). Jesus describes the simple use of what we already have—our go-to senses, eyes and ears—to be attentive and mindful right here, right now. Jesus is not talking about the kind of cluttered, surface awareness that we mindlessly experience through the day. That is merely sensory attention. In fact, Jesus is specifically distinguishing a new kind of awareness: "Those with ears to hear" are those who pay careful attention to a deeper reality, not just whatever surface noise hits their ears.

How would you describe the difference between surface awareness and the awareness that comes from eyes to see and ears to hear the reign of God?

Gospel mindfulness has "eyes to see and ears to hear" this present moment where Jesus speaks into our lives. The prayerful attentiveness of gospel mindfulness perceives what is real and seeks to grasp what really matters. Gospel mindfulness interrupts the running story lines that busy our minds with judgments about others or with obsessive, anxious thoughts.

These running story lines are not Real with a capital *R*. They are ideas we create in our brains to make sense of our experience.

This story-telling to ourselves is an important human strategy. But if we are captive to our mental mixtape, we will miss true Life at this very moment. The Spirit can be speaking into our lives, God can be moving in us, and we will miss it entirely because we are lost in mental machinations.

Jesus calls us to pay attention to the present moment because that is where the reign of God is, in the here and now. He proclaims the kingdom of God—God's sovereign life here and now in us and around us—and then calls us to mindfulness: See! Hear! Be mindful of what is truly real, what truly matters. It's almost as though Jesus were saying, "Have eyes to see and ears to hear this present moment, the reign of God, right here in and around you!"

Jesus urgently calls his followers to grasp this reality ruled by love, already embedded in our lives. Often in the Gospels Jesus describes God's reign as today, near, or at hand: "Now is the time! Here comes God's kingdom!" (Mark 1:15) and "the kingdom of heaven has come near" (Matt 10:7).[3] In the inauguration of his ministry and mission in Luke 4 Jesus claims, "Today, this scripture has been fulfilled just as you heard it" (v. 21), referring to the good news to the poor, release of captives, recovery of sight to the blind, and the day of the Lord's favor. This is not some far-off fantasy, but a present reality that God is enacting.

Jesus also describes mindfulness in his parables about staying awake.[4] Staying awake is a central theme in Jesus's teaching as a metaphor for being spiritually awake to God and God's present kingdom. In a world where so many feel they are sleepwalking through their lives, Jesus's call to be awake resonates with the vague awareness of missing out on our own lives.

Jesus tells stories about people who miss out because they fall asleep. In some stories, sleeping results in missing out on a blessing or celebration. In others, it results in becoming vulnerable to theft or danger. Either way, being awake is Jesus's way of talking about a life awake to what God is up to.

In one story, Jesus tells about ten people in a wedding party. Five fall asleep before the party gets started and miss the celebration entirely (Matt 25:1-13). Jesus contrasts these five with the other five who stay awake and join in the wedding banquet. If we do not intentionally plan to stay awake, we probably won't. Without some plan or preparation, we are likely to miss out on God's party. Being awake is necessary for abundant life.[5]

In the parable of the thief in the night (Matt 24:43-44; Luke 12:39-40) Jesus describes the thief who breaks into the house while the homeowner sleeps. Failure to "stay awake" can mean our lives get stolen out from under us. When we are preoccupied or asleep instead of mindful and awake, we are robbed of our valuables, the very moments so precious to us in the lives of our children, friends, or world.

Beyond these parables, Jesus himself experiences the sleepiness of his followers when his disciples fall asleep in the garden of Gethsemane, just at the time he has asked them to stay awake with him. We hear the disappointment in Jesus's words, "Couldn't you stay alert one hour with me?" (Matt 26:40).

In all these ways, Jesus uses "awake" to describe being aware or attentive or mindful. "Asleep" means unaware, inattentive, or unmindful. When our senses are fully awake, we are aware of the environment around us, of the feel of the air on our cheeks, of sounds near and far, and of our own internal sensations. When we are asleep, we are unaware of all of these things. To intensify the lesson, Jesus sets some stories late at night, when it's hardest to stay awake. We get the message: we need mindfulness the most when our lives become numbed by chronic distractedness or we sleepwalk through our day in a stupor of busy-ness, making us the sleepy ones in Jesus's stories.

Jesus speaks into our daily lives: it may not be too difficult to stay awake to God when we are spiritually rested and alert, but it gets much harder when we are spiritually exhausted and drained by crammed calendars.

In these accounts sleeping itself is not declared wrong. It is a natural physical state. We all need sleep! In fact, neurologists tell us that periods of inattention or mindless spacing out may in fact be helpful for mental function and problem-solving. Jesus's point is that, because sleep is a natural state, we have to be *intentional* to stay awake to God. We pay prayerful attention *on purpose*. That's why Jesus repeats his proclamation so many times that the kingdom of God is at hand, and we will miss it if we don't pay attention.

Jesus points to such *paying attention on purpose* when visiting his friends Mary and Martha (Luke 10:38-42). He sounds like he is speaking directly into our multitasking lives of today when he says to Martha, overwhelmed by her to-do list, "Martha, Martha, you are worried and distracted by many things" (v. 42). He sees Martha's harried countenance, hears the resentment in her voice, and says that worry and distraction are not the way that leads to life. Jesus completely shatters our carefully constructed sense of self-importance bestowed by multitasking and productivity management skills. While our flurry of activity seems Very Important, Jesus says it is not. "One thing is necessary." What? All those tasks aren't necessary? "Mary has chosen the better part." Mary "sat at the Lord's feet and listened to his message" (vv. 42, 39). She was present in that moment with Jesus, attentive and teachable.

8

What Else Does the Bible Say about Mindfulness?

Paul repeats Jesus's call to wakefulness in his letters to early Christian communities to keep awake. Again and again, Paul cautions them to wake up and be alert.[6] He calls them to mindfulness of Christ in order to live a God-accompanied life. Wakeful attentiveness is an essential posture for the converted life.

Moreover, Paul calls us to "pray continually" (1 Thess 5:17), suggesting that prayer is not so much a string of words as a way of being in the world. In this same letter, Paul exhorts Christians to rejoice, give thanks, hold fast to what is good, help the weak, and be at peace with one another. These behaviors rely on prayerful attentiveness so that our walking-around-everyday-lives are unceasing prayer (see Rom 12:2 The Message).

Paul also makes clear that prayer as an orientation of life points us toward Christlikeness. Through mindfulness we learn to see and participate in God's abundant life, the reign of God, in the everyday world. We grow in Christlikeness, having "the same mind be in you that was in Christ" (Phil 2:5 NRSV), that mind that seeks to love others and world.

It's no surprise Jesus, and then Paul, calls us to mindfulness because they were both formed in practices of paying attention to God's abundant life through their own Hebrew tradition. The Hebrew Scriptures are full of passages that call the Hebrew people to mindfulness of God here, now. This call often begins with "Hear, O Israel!" or "Remember, O Israel!" These call the Hebrew people to pay attention to what God has done, is doing, and will do. Remembrance of God's mighty acts in salvation is a form of mindfulness that is encoded in many Hebrew prayers and rituals.

Mindfulness of God's shalom is at the heart of Hebrew faith and practice. Sabbath rest interrupts weekly routines in order to turn awareness to God. The Psalms sing out, turning one's breath and body toward God. In Psalm 46, God instructs the Israelites in this practice: "Be still, and know that I am God!" (Ps 46:10 NRSV). The prophet Isaiah warns against the danger of seeing yet not understanding, of listening yet not perceiving (Isa 6:9-10; 29:10). Only paying prayerful attention can turn seeing and hearing into understanding and perceiving.

The story of Elijah's experience of God's presence on Mount Horeb illustrates the attentive posture of mindfulness toward God in Hebrew tradition (1 Kgs 19:1-17). As Elijah stands on the mountain watching for God, he experiences a fierce wind, an earthquake, and a fire. God is not in any of these. Finally, in sheer silence, a silence so powerful Elijah covers his face with his mantle, he is able to know God's presence. Only in the pause for silence does he hear God's "still small voice" (v. 12 KJV) or "gentle whisper" (v. 12 NIV).

Jesus Meets People Where They Are, Right Here, Right Now

In his ministry of teaching and healing, Jesus embodies the claim that God is at work in this present moment. In the Gospels, when Jesus encounters people, he always meets them where they are, usually in their need. Especially in healing stories, Jesus meets people where they are in their illness or condition. He doesn't say to them, "Get clean first and then we'll talk." He doesn't ask them when they last went to church or read their Bible. He puts no doctrinal test or moral requirement as a hurdle to his presence.

No, he steps into their reality, accepting where they are, whatever condition they are in, in order to offer his healing presence.

Gospel mindfulness counts on this. When we stop, notice what we are experiencing, and accept it with open hearts and minds, we allow Jesus to meet us there, right where we are.

How does Jesus meet you where you are? Have you experienced this, or does Jesus seem far off? Notice the sensations and feelings that arise in you at this question.

This is God's way. Throughout the Bible God meets people right where they are. In fact, unlike many other gods in the ancient Near East who resided in a particular place, temple, or shrine, the God of the Israelites lived in a movable tabernacle. This God lives in a tent! That's how much this God longed to be with them wherever they were, traveling along. So, when the Gospel of John says that "the Word became flesh and made his home among us" (John 1:14), it could instead be translated, "The Word became flesh and set up a tent to live with us." The Message translates it, "The Word...moved into the neighborhood." This is a God who wants to be right where we are, not off on a cloud somewhere, but right here, right now, with us.

Distinctives: What Is Christian about Christian Mindfulness?

Remember, we said that Christian mindfulness is *paying prayerful attention in the present moment to God's abundant life.* So what's Christian about it? As Christians, our biblical understandings of

God, humanity, the world and the life of faith shape our practice of mindfulness. When we practice mindfulness, we do so as followers of Jesus, as ones who believe in the living God active here in our midst. And that matters.

First, as Christians, we have an incarnated view of life. That means we believe God is present and working in all things, including each of us. This is a surprisingly radical claim. Too often, God is portrayed as remote, watching from afar, or off on a cloud. This leaves the impression that God is off somewhere waiting for us to get our act together or go to church or pray correctly in order to show up in our lives. Christian mindfulness claims the opposite—that God is here now, in all things at all times, even when we aren't paying attention. Our Scripture proclaims, "You know when I sit down and when I stand up... [and are] thoroughly familiar with all my ways" (Ps 139:2-3) and, "The Word became flesh and lived among us" (John 1:14 NRSV). Stop and let this sink in. The good news of Jesus Christ is that God is with us, no matter what, no matter where, no matter when. There is no place you can go where God is not, no time of the day when God is off the clock. This is the teaching of the Incarnation, God with us; this very present God active in all creation, in all human life.

How has God been portrayed to you? What is your primary image of God? Notice the sensations or feelings that arise in you at this question.

Second, as Christians, we believe that humans are bodies, souls, and minds all bound up in one whole together. We are not dualists. We do not believe that our bodies are bad and our spirits

are good. Or that God works through a spiritual realm while ignoring our bodies in the physical realm. Remember: this is the
God *who became flesh* and lived among us. Far from rejecting the
body, Christianity embraces human embodiment as blessed by
God in the Incarnation. It follows, then, that we fully embrace
our bodies as part of our spiritual lives, as one of the ways God
meets us where we are, a source of revelation where God is at
work.

So, for Christians, mindfulness practice always begins with
awareness of our bodies, sensations that arise, our emotions and
thoughts. We begin by attending to our immediate, physical experience. For example, we become aware of tension in our shoulders
or tiredness in our calves or tightness in our face muscles. Some
of us perceive emotions first in our bodies, perhaps resentment
about a coworker or awe about a mother holding hands with her
child. We focus on this concrete experience *in our bodies* first.

Third, as Christians we understand that human beings are
finite, limited in our ability to know ourselves, the world, and
God. We are prone to self-absorption and forgetfulness of God.
We become captive to our own particular life stories, our wounds
and brokenness. Or, conversely, we congratulate ourselves on the
lives we have built and credit ourselves with all we have. The great
spiritual teachers throughout Christian history remind us that we
need help to stay awake to God, that on our own we too easily
become lost, in ourselves or in the world's expectations. Therefore,
we need practices and patterns of life that free us for God.

Therefore, as Christians, mindfulness is not some generic practice as an end in itself, but a practice that turns us toward God.
The New Testament word *metanoia* describes turning our minds
and our lives to God. We often translate *metanoia* as "repentance,"

an English word that tends to convey an emotional state of regret more than the active state of change. Christian mindfulness is a practice of daily turning, of *metanoia*, turning our finite, prone-to-forgetfulness minds to God, of "be[ing] transformed by the renewing of your minds" (Rom 12:2). Or, as The Message translation offers, "Take your everyday, ordinary life—your sleeping, eating, going-to-work, and walking-around life—and place it before God.... You'll be changed from the inside out."

The *metanoia* of Christian mindfulness leads to our fourth point on what is Christian about Christian mindfulness. While mindfulness practice always begins with awareness of our bodies, it doesn't end there. The purpose of Christian mindfulness is not only body-awareness but God-awareness. When we stop and pay attention to our concrete experience right now, we sink more deeply into this present moment and allow the surface clutter to float away. As our mindfulness roots us more deeply right here, right now, we have eyes to see and ears to hear God. We wake up not only to ourselves but also to God's life in us and in the world around us. This God who "moved into the neighborhood" has been here all along, often held at arm's length by the clutter that distracts our attention. We become mindful of the One who made us and Who holds us within God's own life.

This brings us full circle back to the first point above. As Christians we proclaim God is present in all things. Therefore, our experiences of God are not reserved for church or for "spiritual" moments. God doesn't show up only in prayer or Bible reading or in heaven after we die. God is present when we are sitting at the stoplight, helping kids with homework, and in that frustrating meeting at work. God is working in those brief sentences with my spouse before we head out the door, at my yoga class, and

14

when I'm surfing online. My entire mundane, daily, messy life rests in God. All of it. The more I practice mindfulness, the more I become aware of God, the True Life that holds my life in this moment. The goal of Christian mindfulness is God-awareness, an experience of our lives in God, our true home. Jesus says it, "Look! See! The kingdom of God is at hand!" Christian mindfulness cultivates this seeing.

How do you see the kingdom of God at hand, right here, right now?

Lastly, let's remember that we are not the only ones being mindful. God is mindful of *us*. Psalm 139 above expresses how God is mindful of each of our lives in each moment, when we sit down and when we rise. The psalmist asks, "What are human beings that you think about them...that you pay attention to them?" (Ps 8:4). Our God pays attention, is mindful on both the cosmic and the quantum levels. We take comfort that on those days when our own mindfulness practice falters, God's mindfulness is always faithful, sheltering us in the Divine Triune Life.

Marks of Christian Mindfulness: How Does Mindfulness Mark Our Lives?

We can expect to experience real differences in our lives as a result of practicing gospel mindfulness. The Christian life is not an idea, a disembodied set of thoughts one must think each day. The Christian life is a *way* of life, a way of being and doing in the world. In fact, the New Testament calls it "the way." That means we take up practices and patterns of life, like mindfulness, through which we are formed more and more into Christlikeness, and, with God, bear fruit for the world.

Mindfulness practice actually changes our minds, changes our brains and consciousness over time. It is self-reinforcing. Our neuro-pathways are rutted with conditioned reactions and responses. Mindfulness practice rewires these rutted neuro-pathways, creating new ones. These actual physical changes in our brains and bodies begin to mark our lives in concrete ways.

Christian mindfulness offers many benefits, including improved mental and physical health, better discernment of God's voice, and a deeper spiritual life. Here I want to highlight five marks of mindful Christian lives that are particularly important for a fast-paced and overstimulated life.

We Are Free

When we practice Christian mindfulness, our lives become more free. This takes several forms. Perhaps the most powerful form is freedom from reactivity. As we practice Christian mindfulness consistently over time, we find that indeed we are not so much "conformed to the patterns of this world" (Rom 12:2). That is, we are less reactive in our daily lives, freed from knee-jerk responses to triggers or obsessive anxieties. In mindful awareness we stop and notice internal reactions, giving ourselves space to hold our reactions lightly, to become curious and kind with ourselves and to look for God's presence.

We live in a world inflamed by reactivity. From constant social media to around-the-clock newsfeeds, we live in a culture of reactivity, ready to pounce with outrage on the latest headline or quote, regardless of how much real information we have. This form of reactivity is especially dangerous in the Christian life, because the self-righteousness that often accompanies outrage can feel so good. It feels good to be right and point my finger at those people who are wrong. Mindfulness practice interrupts this reactivity, first by gathering concrete information about what is happening in my body in this moment and then by choosing to act, rather than react, with intentionality. Lives marked by freedom offer a powerful corrective to a reactive culture, a Christian witness to the good news, a way to not "be conformed to the patterns of this world" (Rom 12:2).

Often reactivity is fueled by fear, a toxin to the Christian witness in the world. Mindful Christian lives are marked by freedom from fear, the opposite of faith. Scripture tells us over and over, "Be not afraid." Nowhere does Jesus say we will be known by our fear, yet that is precisely what many Christians are known by today. Instead, Jesus says we will be known by our love (John 13:35).

As we live lives more free *from* reactivity and the chronic anxiety it feeds, we become free *for* greater clarity and agency in our lives, another way freedom marks our lives. "Christ has set us free for freedom. Therefore, stand firm and don't submit to the bondage of slavery again" (Gal 5:1). There are many kinds of yokes, and mindless submission to the incessant distractions of the world around us is one of them. Christ frees us from this yoke, drawing our attention to God's life and work in us. With practice over time, we can see our true lives more clearly in this moment, in focus rather than blurred. This clarity can free us to act, to make choices in this moment about who we will be and how we will pour out our lives for the world in Jesus's name.

Another way our lives can be marked by freedom is that we are free *for* recognizing God's voice in our lives. Most of us have many internal voices as well as external voices competing for our attention. It can be hard to listen for God when both our self-talk and the onslaught of outer demands jam all the signals. Which of these are of God? Which warrant our attention and consideration? Through mindfulness we come to recognize God speaking into our lives. As we are free to hear God's voice in the present moment we better discern God's desire for our lives and also for the world God so loves. Christian mindfulness frees up bandwidth for "the renewing of our minds," which Paul says has the goal of discerning God's desire: "be transformed by the renewing of your minds so that you can figure out what God's will is" (Rom 12:2). Such freedom roots us in God's deepest desires.

What voice most often dominates your internal conversation? Notice the sensations or feelings that arise in you at this question.

We Are Real

Christian mindfulness marks our lives with authenticity. One of the hungers of our time is for authentic lives. By that, most people mean lives that are real, not fake. We lead fake lives when we try to be something we aren't, hide our real selves, or carefully craft the image we project to others. The constant maintenance of pretense is exhausting, and we are often not even aware we are doing it. Grasping for the next sign of success or approval leaves us empty, focused always on the future and unable to see our real lives here, now. In contrast, authentic lives are the actual, messy lives we have in this moment, without pretense or masks.

In mindfulness practice we stop to let God name our real lives. As we pay prayerful attention in the present moment, false masks fall away so that we can see the life we actually have. We may not like what we discover, but it is the starting place for the abundant life God offers.

Being real opens up not only our own lives but also lives around us. Being real is a countercultural way of living that invites others to do the same. You know this from your own experience of being drawn to those who live authentically, those who are willing to be themselves truly without pretense, to share their vulnerabilities undefended. We are drawn to such folks because we, too, hunger for authentic lives. Their witness is an invitation to stop propping up fake versions of ourselves and instead inhabit the real, true life we have. Our authentic lives will be just this sort of invitation to others, a way of being the good news.

To be sure, Christian mindfulness does not magically produce authentic lives. We are always capable of ignoring or denying what mindfulness reveals. In order to be real we must choose to acknowledge honestly and prayerfully whatever arises. That's why attending to God's presence is so critical for Christian mindfulness. As we learn to see our lives in this moment held in God's loving arms, we spend less time and energy projecting our false selves and instead inhabit more deeply our authentic lives in God.

We Are Rooted

A third way Christian mindfulness marks our lives is that we are rooted, more centered. Think about lives that are scattered in a flurry of tasks throughout the day, as we multitask several things simultaneously. This fragmentation leaves folks feeling adrift, untethered to anything and therefore subject to whatever winds happen to be strongest today. Moreover, it takes a lot of energy to move through daily life from one thing to the next without a sense that all the things connect. One parent described it as carrying around an armload of random puzzle pieces that don't fit together while new random pieces show up.

In contrast, Christian mindfulness roots us in a center that holds, cohering the pieces together. As we stop to pay attention prayerfully to the present moment, we root our lives in God's abundant life, the true center that holds our lives together. It is not our job to create wholeness in our lives, but to rest in the wholeness God provides. Mindfulness practice nourishes this root, cultivating "eyes to see" and "ears to hear" our true center.

We Are Grateful

A fourth mark of mindfulness is gratitude. Gratitude is a powerful corrective to corrosive messages that whatever we have and whatever we are is not enough. Under the weight of this barrage, we compare ourselves with others and fall prey to consumer fantasies of the good life. We become convinced that our current lives fall short, so we must work harder and faster to have more, do more, and be more. We even pressure our children into this narrative, overscheduling their lives to ensure they, too, measure up.

In contrast, Christian mindfulness draws our attention to what we actually have in this moment, starting with our breath. Each breath is a complete gift, not something we create, produce, or earn. With awareness of each breath that fills our lungs, of each steady heartbeat, we become grateful for the sheer gift of life itself in this moment. We start to see the simple things we have mindlessly taken for granted, like clean drinking water or safe shelter.

Our gratitude deepens as we see more and more what we have rather than what we don't have. The good news of abundant life in Christ is that the world's messages of "not enough" are a lie. Still, these messages are so constant and so loud that if we are not mindful, we will miss the truth that our lives are already full to overflowing with blessing. With practice, we become grateful for the flourishing of God's life here, now, in front of us.

Our Hearts Open to Others

Another way mindfulness marks our lives is that our hearts open to others. We are more able to live with and for our neighbors. Compassion marks our lives as we are free, real, rooted, and grateful. Mindful in the present moment of God's abundant life and our participation with what God is up to in the world, our hearts expand, overflowing for others. In fact, this is exactly what Jesus means by "abundant" life. He's not talking about the abundance of conspicuous consumption, a big screen TV or a new car every year. The Greek word here is *perisson*, meaning superfluous or full to overflowing. Living abundantly means our lives overflow with God's love for the world, not an abstract idea, but in concrete actions, in this particular moment. Compassion is the ground of action in the world.

Compassion is hard when we are distracted and preoccupied, when we are more likely to be irritable than compassionate, frustrated than patient, quick to judge than attentive to the layers of reality in front of us. In fact, when our brains get overloaded, in an attempt at efficiency they default to quick, superficial judgments, putting people in preexisting boxes. We reduce others to shorthand: soccer mom, tattooed biker, troubled teen, old white guy. As we are free to really see what was a blur before, as we are real about our own lives, our hearts open to the harried mom in front of us at the checkout, who is no longer an obstacle stalling the line but a precious child of God struggling to make ends meet. Our hearts expand, overflowing with compassion as we see the world through God's eyes of love. We can act, rather than react, with greater purpose toward justice, mercy, and healing in Jesus's name.

There's a bit of a domino effect here. Being real means we get more comfortable in our own skin, more ready to accept ourselves on a daily basis. Correspondingly, we are more able to accept others as they are, too. The more we recognize our own creatureliness as human beings, with all the weakness and insecurity that entails, the more we see the beauty of this common humanity in others. We experience compassion for all God's children when we pay prayerful attention in this moment to God's abundant life. We live toward less suffering and more mercy. Compassion insists that Christian mindfulness is not for ourselves only but always for the world that God loves.

Abundant Life

Being free, real, rooted, grateful, and openhearted for others are only some of the ways Christian mindfulness can mark our lives. There are many more you will discover. Moreover, Christians use differing vocabularies as tools to help describe these marks. One vocabulary is "fruits," or "fruit of the Spirit": "love, joy, peace, patience, kindness, goodness, faithfulness, gentleness, and self-control" (Gal 5:22-23). Paul describes these as fruit because they grow from one's life in God. This is not a checklist to be achieved, but real-life experiences that sprout up in our day, usually surprising us as gifts of grace. For example, perhaps I am able to be patient with my coworker or at peace in the face of uncertainty. Spiritual practices cultivate fruits as the Spirit changes our lives and changes the world.

Another traditional language to describe the marks of the Christian life is "growing into Christlikeness," the whole point of our Christian walk. This is the daily *metanoia* of the converted life, being transformed in each moment. Our lives are renewed as we "let the same mind be in you that was in Christ Jesus" (Phil 2:5 NRSV). While some may be intimidated by the thought of Christlikeness, this is always the work of God in us, a concrete fruit of paying attention to our lives in God.

Finally, one shorthand to describe the marks of a mindful life is simply "abundant life," Jesus's words for the life he is offering. Jesus offers us this free, real, rooted, grateful, openhearted life in every moment. Yet we miss the invitation when we are preoccupied and distracted. If we pay attention instead, we can live abundantly, loving God with our whole heart, soul, mind, and strength, and our neighbors as ourselves. The spiritual practice of Christian mindfulness issues in fidelity to God's love. This is the good news of abundant life in Christ.

What marks of mindfulness do you most long for in your life right now?

Conclusion

In chapter 1, we have laid the biblical and theological foundations for the practice of Christian mindfulness. Christian mindfulness is *paying prayerful attention in the present moment to God's abundant life.* Jesus teaches a gospel mindfulness that has eyes to see and ears to hear the kingdom of God at hand. As Christians our biblical faith shapes our understanding and practice of mindfulness. The marks of Christian mindfulness are real and benefit not only ourselves but also the world God loves. In the next chapter, we will look at the ways mindfulness shows up throughout Christian tradition and on the cultural landscape today.

For Further Reading

Gospel of Matthew, Gospel of Mark, Gospel of Luke, Gospel of John

McHugh, Adam S., *The Listening Life: Embracing Attentiveness in a World of Distraction* (Downers Grove, Ill.: InterVarsity, 2015).

Chapter 2

Curating Mindfulness in Christian Tradition and Contemporary Culture

Having identified some foundational aspects of Christian mindfulness in chapter 1, now we turn to the ways mindfulness shows up in the history of Christian spirituality and in the world around us.

Curating Mindfulness: Why It Matters

As Christians, we have an interesting relationship to the world. We are "in the world but not of it," that is, we are called to love the world that "God so loves" without conforming to its expectations and values.[1] Christian leaders in particular are called upon to read the culture, to understand and interpret cultural movements and trends, in order to help Christian communities love the world without being conformed to it. This work is a kind of "curating," a process of faithful seeing and prayerful living.

The missional life of the church depends on Christians curating our own tradition and the larger culture we swim in if we want to live by the biblical promise that God has already "moved into the neighborhood" (John 1:14 The Message).[2] We curate the culture, albeit critically, to see what God is up to in the world, to participate in the *missio Dei*. The incarnate God meets us in the very culture we inhabit, seeking to redeem and restore the world that is subject to human corruption.

Do you agree that Christians are called to love the world without conforming to it? How would you describe this posture in your life?

This task of curating is not private. It is an ongoing communal project within the body of Christ, something we have done for centuries, with the guidance of the Holy Spirit. For example, the movement to abolish slavery in the United States illustrates Christians curating tradition, sifting through inherited interpretations of Scripture, as well as paying attention to fresh perspectives in the culture, in order to witness faithfully to the good news.

One cannot survey the current cultural landscape without spotting the mindfulness movement, widespread and well documented.[3] We encounter it at work, yoga class, and in the news. Mindfulness is a formative practice that shapes many people's daily lives, often outside of church. It may be that mindfulness practice offers a spiritual "safe space," a doorway to spiritual practice for many folks, religious or not. Mindfulness practice may be one place God has "moved into the neighborhood," meeting people where they are in the spiritual hunger of our time.

> *Do you know anyone who practices mindful-*
> *ness? Why do they practice it?*

To get on board with God's mission in the world, Christians must be curators, both of our own tradition and of the larger cultural landscape. Part 1 of this chapter surveys Christian spiritual traditions that incorporate mindfulness, and part 2 looks at the mindfulness movement in many segments of society today.

Part 1: Mindfulness in Christian Tradition

Vocabulary of Prayer

Part of the widespread confusion about whether mindfulness is a Christian practice comes from our varied vocabulary for prayer. Christians use words like *petition, confession,* or *praise* to identify prayer types. We often talk about contemplative, intercessory, or liturgical prayer, but few have heard of mindfulness prayer as a specific name for a Christian practice. As a result, many assume mindfulness is not present within our Christian witness. Yet *paying prayerful attention* is an emphasis throughout the history of Christian spirituality, so mindfulness actually shows up a lot.

> *In what forms of prayer are you most at home?*
> *How do prayer and mindfulness connect for*
> *you?*

Mindfulness is another word for prayerful attention to God's presence right here, right now. Contemplative traditions within Christianity have always emphasized attentive awareness of God

27

in this moment, using various words, including *prayer* and *meditation*. Historically, Christians have used many practices of mindfulness, drawing on the biblical witness of attentive presence with God, for example, "Be still, and know that I am God!" (Ps 46:10 NRSV), "a sound of sheer silence" (1 Kgs 19:12 NRSV), "Mary treasured all these words and pondered them in her heart" (Luke 2:19 NRSV), and "pray continually" (1 Thess 5:17). It may help to remember that prayer is an organic expression of our relationship with God, taking many forms in Scripture and across Christian history.

Part 1 of this chapter will identify some ways mindfulness weaves through Christian tradition and practice. For instructions on practices, see chapter 3.

Early Christianity

The great spiritual teachers of early Christianity made the radical move to the outposts of empire, the desert, in order to create communities of mindfulness. These mothers and fathers of the early desert movement developed spiritual practices that focus on loving God and neighbor. Desert Christians were mindful of the fierce spiritual struggle present both "in here" in our hearts and "out there" in the world.[4] Disciples would ask their *abba* or *amma* to "give me a word," to break through the mental clutter to return one's awareness to God, making room for love.

Many of these desert Christians, including Evagrius Ponticus (345–399 CE) and his student, John Cassian (360–435 CE), teach that prayer is rooted first in mindful awareness of God already present if we will only stop and pay attention.[5] The key operative principle is *apatheia*, a simple *being* in God's presence without preoccupations or unconscious drives pulling us this way and that.[6] Evagrius was concerned to counter the numbing effects of an overstimulated life, mentally scattered and out of touch with any spiritual center. *Apatheia* frees us for mindful attention to God's deepest desires for us. Such freedom from distraction opens up space to see and hear God's abundant life in and around us.

A key component of early desert spirituality was the cell, a small, enclosed space, usually a small cave or room made of stacked rocks, where desert Christians would retreat throughout the day to pause and pay attention to God without external distractions. The cell was a strategy for Christian mindfulness that inevitably revealed to the seeker the present moment in their own hearts, often framed as spiritual battle. The outer cell served as portal to the inner heart. Athanasius's *Life of St. Anthony* (c. 251–356) documents the spiritual encounters of the cell where Anthony focused his attention on God and was transformed. When asked "give me a word," the desert mothers and fathers would often direct their students to their cells wherein, through paying attention to God, they could hear the true word speaking to their own spiritual confusion or communal squabbles. "A brother came to Scetis to visit Abba Moses and asked him for a word. The old man said to him, 'Go, sit in your cell and your cell will teach you everything.'"[7]

Early Christians also practiced *nepsis*, a watchfulness of heart and mind, as foundational for the Christian life. The New Testament (1 Pet 5:8) uses the verb *nepho* to describe a spiritual posture that is awake and mindful. *Nepsis* is a posture alert to the knowing of the heart, where God's wisdom resides. This wakefulness orders awareness, allowing one to become alert to the pitfalls of intellectual grasping on the one hand, and self-sufficient life management on the other. Instead, it listens for God's speaking into our lives, a noetic perception attuned to God. Because one of the greatest impediments to this listening is our dulled numbness from sensory overload, *nepsis* is intended to help us wake up to God. St. Gregory of Sinai sounds eerily aware of our postmodern experience when he says that our lives have been "overlaid by a state of sense-dominated mindlessness," which sounds like the numbed fog one gets from hours of net-surfing![8] *Nepsis* is the posture awake to our true life in God and thus less vulnerable to the stupor of robotic busy-ness and bombarding sensory input.

Early Christians held vigils as they gathered to watch and pray, most often at death and on the eve of holy days. The word *vigilant* comes from *vigil* and conveys the intensity of this practice. To watch and pray entailed staying awake through the night (later ritualized in the funeral wake) both to be present with the deceased and to anticipate the promise of resurrection in the Christian burial rite the following day. The vigil was not merely passing time in prayer but being watchful for God in expectation and hope. This recalls Jesus's instructions not merely to pray but to watch, in attentive expectation of God's presence. The vigil interrupted employment, family life, and even religious commitments to call the Christian community to mindful attention of God's presence here now in the midst of death and life. Many ancient records give witness to this mindful practice, notably Gregory of Nyssa's *Life of Macrina the Younger*, as he reports the influx of crowds to sing psalms through the night vigil upon the death of his older sister and spiritual teacher.

Similarly, on the eve of holy days and particularly on Holy Saturday before Easter, Christians held vigil to pause and turn complete attention to what God is doing. The vigil marked the threshold of entering holy time with one's full being given to watching for God. This watching entails staying awake as distractions and preoccupations of the day fall away and all one's senses are alert in expectation. More than clocking time, the vigil cultivates "eyes to see" and "ears to hear" the kingdom of God at hand through paying prayerful attention.[9]

The Jesus prayer is another example of a historical practice intent on focusing awareness on our present lives in God. Originating in the earliest centuries of Christianity, the Jesus prayer became widely practiced in eastern Orthodox devotion, especially among the Hesychasts in the seventh and eighth centuries. This prayer uses focused breathing and the phrase "Jesus Christ, Son of God, have mercy on me." Beginning with mindfulness of our present state, including honest awareness of our need for mercy, the Jesus prayer claims Christ's continual presence with us here, now. This prayer practice was later championed in "The Way of the Pilgrim" as a way to see Jesus present with us in every step.[10]

Benedict of Nursia, the founder of Benedictine monasticism, was influenced by the principles of both *apatheia* and *nepsis* in early Christianity. Early monastic communities observed the divine offices, set hours for communal prayer, in recognition that humans need intentional, even institutionalized, structures to exercise mindfulness in the Christian life. *The Rule of Benedict* offers one of the very early iterations of this practice.

The Rule of Benedict sets out the practice of praying the eight canonical hours. These were intended to punctuate daily life so that both physical work and attention to God were woven into one fluid whole. These fixed times of communal prayer were an expression of Benedict's call to "work and pray," insisting that God was not outside the rhythms of daily life, but very much embedded within them. Set times to pause and recognize God in the midst of work was a form of mindfulness of life in God.

31

Without such structural aids to stop and pay attention, the daily grind can make us numb and insensible to God's working in us. Benedict alludes to the seduction of busy-ness and the idol of productivity when he declares, "*Nothing* is to be preferred above the work of God" (chapter 43).[11] Therefore, in Benedict's community, when a monk hears the bell for the divine office, no matter how pressing the task before him, he turns his heart to God. In this way, the divine offices train our eyes to see God in all things, including and especially the mundane.

The early Christian practice of *lectio divina*, or holy reading, offered a countercultural method of reading in the late Roman world and indeed in our own. In this practice, instead of reading to "get something out of it," Christians read to be *with* God in this moment, to pay prayerful attention to God's presence in Scripture. This approach is different than reading for information or to settle a doctrinal dispute. *Lectio divina* slows down Bible reading, encouraging pauses to be *with*, rather than to gain mastery over, Scripture. This leisurely approach cultivates awareness both of God's presence here now in these words and in our lives. This practice began in monastic communities and over the centuries spread into lay and congregational practices.

The early Christian world is full of on-the-ground life practices that draw attention to God in the present moment, more than we can cover here. Let's look briefly at one more: the prayer of St. Patrick (fifth century), "Christ before me, Christ behind me." The Celtic stream of Christian spirituality attends to our embodied lives in creation, concerned with the here and now, always ready to encounter Christ. The record of St. Patrick's prayer illustrates this, naming Christ's presence right here, right now, in all dimensions of time and space—above, below, in front, behind, inside, and out. In praying this prayer, one cannot help becoming mindful in this moment of Christ concretely with us.

Medieval Christianity

Medieval Christians were hungry to connect to God directly as the church became more hierarchical and theology more complex. Medieval Christian life flourishes with spiritual practices that engage the senses in embodied mindfulness. Icons draw the visual senses into an encounter with the divine. Shrines and relics give concrete physicality to connecting with God in a particular place. Pilgrimage puts one's feet squarely on a holy path expecting to encounter God. Praying the rosary brings one's hands into action, paying prayerful attention with the touch of each bead. Stained glass windows, incense, and soaring architecture all draw the senses into mindful awareness of God's presence here and now. All these physical prompts use the body to pay prayerful attention in the present moment to God's movement.

The "modern devotion" movement of the fourteenth century is an another witness of a grassroots movement within the Christian tradition of mindfulness of daily, embodied life with God. This largely lay movement turned away from dogmatic scholasticism, on the one hand, and away from ecclesiastical machinations, on the other, to focus entirely on the Christian walk of shared life in God.[12] They created intentional communities of humility and simplicity so they could pay prayerful attention to God present in their midst, not far off on a cloud somewhere. These lay communities of men and women read Scripture, prayed the divine offices, served neighbors, and observed solitary time with God. They sought a deep, authentic faith that was practiced in the world, mindful of God right here, right now.

Mindfulness of the glory of God sings through the work of Francis of Assisi (1181–1226), founder of the Franciscan tradition.[13] The well-known "Canticle of Brother Sun" conveys the joy of simple awareness in the present moment of each aspect of creation, claiming each as a family member (brother sun, sister moon, etc.). For Francis, every breath, every sip of water, every creature, every ray of light offered testimony to the powerful, present work of God. Pausing to pay attention and give thanks punctuated his community's life of simplicity and poverty. Both the Franciscans and the Poor Clares, a women's order, preached good news and lived in solidarity with the poor, in stark contrast to the ostentatious wealth of many church leaders of the thirteenth century. Francis proclaimed that every present thing in the natural world invites us into God's abundant life.

The so-called mystical tradition of medieval Christian spirituality is rich and well documented. Unfortunately, contemporary usage often renders the word *mystical* as ethereal and otherworldly, escaping the realities of everyday life. Medieval mysticism is not indulged escapism; far from it. Perhaps better called "experiential" spirituality, these Christians sought to engage the presence of God here and now through their bodies and through the world around them, using a wide range of attentive practices from Scripture to ecstatic visions to silent prayer. Experiential mystics, such as Hildegard of Bingen, Julian of Norwich, Meister Eckhart, and the author of *The Cloud of Unknowing*, focus prayerful attention in the present moment on God in and through all things. Julian of Norwich (c. 1342–1416) offers the simple example of gazing on a hazelnut in the palm of her hand to bring mindful awareness of God's presence and sustaining love for all creation, even this smallest and seemingly insignificant part.

Early Modern Christianity

Ignatius of Loyola (1491–1556), the founder of the Society of Jesus (Jesuits) and author of the *Spiritual Exercises*, developed spiritual practices that pay attention to our concrete experience of daily life in order to encounter God. Through his own spiritual journey he had learned that God is at work not only in religious ceremonies or objects, but in our daily experiences, mundane life right in front of us. The Ignatian tradition describes this attentive way of life as "finding God in all things and all things in God."[14] The whole of Ignatius's *Spiritual Exercises* relies on the premise that everything in life, the nitty-gritty details of daily living, opens the path into deeper communion with God. But we must be mindful of it to benefit, to cultivate a God-awareness, a God-accompanied life.

The practice of paying prayerful attention to our lives in God takes several traditional forms in the Ignatian tradition. First, the Examen is a daily exercise in paying attention and honing our perceptions of where and how God is showing up. Second, the *Spiritual Exercises* are a structured, intensive retreat focused on daily mindfulness for Jesus in Scripture and in our lives. The third practice is discernment and decision-making, which require mature mindfulness in order to discern God's desire for a particular circumstance. These are time-tested tools for mindfulness in the Ignatian tradition.

Teresa of Avila (1515–82), and others, taught the prayer of recollection, a way of being mindful of the astonishing reality of God's continual presence with us. The word *recollect* here means to re-collect, or gather together our senses to focus our spiritual center. That's where we dwell with God at this very moment and hard to do when our attention is diffused and distracted. Through the prayer of recollection one returns to God at the center and becomes mindful of "this little heaven of my soul," as Teresa puts it.[15] John of the Cross (1542–91) also promotes the prayer of recollection adding, "It is a matter of great contentment and joy for you to see that He is so near you as to be within you. Rejoice and be glad in your inward recollection with Him, since you have Him so near."[16]

Brother Lawrence (1614–91), author of *The Practice of the Presence of God*,[17] was a monk whose life was so infused with continual mindfulness of God that he inspired others to also "practice the presence of God." No matter how busy one's day is with chores or serving others or even with religious duties, Brother Lawrence says we must stop and become aware, in the present moment, of God right here, right now. As he worked in the kitchen he would frequently pause, just for a moment, to "practice the presence of God" so as to be filled with joy.

Quakers (Society of Friends) have rooted their entire spiritual tradition in the basic practice of "seeking God's light within," mindful awareness of God here and now, manifest through the Inner Light. Friends gather to pay prayerful attention in silence, quieting the surface clutter so that one's senses are free to perceive the light within and among the community. Begun in the 1600s under the leadership of George Fox, the simplicity of Quaker spirituality has promoted its persistence and growth. The weekly meeting is still practiced among many Friends as a time to sit together in silence, mindful of the Inner Light in expectant waiting upon God.[18]

Wesley and Watchfulness

The Methodist and Wesleyan branches of Christianity also include mindfulness. John Wesley (1703–91), the founder of the

Methodist movement, promoted "watchfulness," a spiritual posture alert to God in all things.[19] For Wesley, the Christian life is nothing if not intentional and purposeful, otherwise we will default into spiritual sleepiness. He calls upon Christians who truly want to deepen their life in God to be ever watchful, going so far as to list watchfulness as a general means of grace. While Wesley does not use the word *mindfulness* for this Christian posture, he clearly has in mind a way of life prayerfully attentive to the sensible working of God in every moment. Interestingly, Wesley read Brother Lawrence and included "the practice of the presence of God" in the general means of grace.[20]

Wesley echoes the Christian mindfulness tradition when he says that watchfulness is an "earnest, constant, persevering exercise…yea, the mighty exertion of all the affections of the soul that a [hu]man is capable of. In all things—Whatever you are doing, yet in that, and in all things, watch."[21] Such prayerful attention is a 360-degree, whole-life endeavor.

Wesley was all too aware of the ways daily life is numbing, lulling people into behaviors that garner the world's approval while eating away their souls, or falling into rote religion, just going through the motions at church. Watchfulness was Wesley's way to describe that level of conscious awareness that is awake to the present moment of our lives where God meets us.

As a pastoral leader, Wesley prescribed watchfulness for many common obstacles to an authentic spiritual life. Ever the practical theologian, Wesley advises watchfulness as corrective to those gone astray, on the one hand, and as reinforcement to those on a righteous path, on the other. For example, for those "still wanting in seriousness," that is, those who don't want to ask hard questions of themselves or dig deep, Wesley advises them to be more watchful as a strategy to greater ownership of their spiritual life.[22] In another example, Wesley promotes watchfulness as a method for "avoiding formality" that keeps God and others at arm's length in prayer or conversation, never risking the intimacy of authentic faith.[23]

At the other end of the religious spectrum, watchfulness is a guide to those who think they have attained entire sanctification, that state whereby the Spirit completely transforms a person by love. Because we can so easily misdiagnose ourselves, Wesley advises anyone who claims entire sanctification to "watch always that God may search the ground of their hearts."[24]

Perhaps most important, Wesley claims that watchfulness, as a general means of grace, is expected to produce fruit. It makes a tangible difference in the practitioner's life, so we neglect watchfulness at our peril. Hear his astounding claim about watching, "Do you endeavor to set God always before you? To see his eye continually fixed upon you? Never can you use these means [of grace] but a blessing will ensue. And the more you use them the more will you grow in grace."[25] Blessings will inevitably come from attentive mindfulness with God, right here, right now.

Wesley's whole ministry emphasized accountable, intentional faith. It's no surprise that a mindful practice such as watchfulness is woven throughout his preaching and teaching.

Part 1 shows how the practice of Christian mindfulness has been woven throughout Christian history, in multiple forms and with varying vocabularies. In part 2 we turn to mindfulness in postmodern life.

Which Christian spiritual traditions of part 1 resonate for you?

Part 2: Mindfulness in Contemporary Culture

Part 2 maps the most visible points of the mindfulness movement in America today, from automakers to professional athletes. The pervasive practice of mindfulness signals, in part, the deep hunger many people have for a practical way to center their lives amid fragmentation and scattered attention. The rapid spread of mindfulness practice also points to its simplicity as easily adaptable to many contexts. Best-selling books have popularized mindfulness practice.[26] Part 2 will highlight the mindfulness movement evident in the behavioral sciences, neuroscience, education, business, sports, and yoga.

Behavioral Sciences

Many people are introduced to mindfulness practice in a therapeutic setting. The list of therapies that incorporate mindfulness practice is long. Perhaps most well known and widely used is mindful-based stress reduction (MBSR). Others include mindfulness-based cognitive therapy (MBCT), dialectic behavioral therapy (DBT), mindfulness-based relapse prevention (MBRP), acceptance commitment therapy (ACT), conduct disorder treatment, and treatment of PTSD, to name only a few.[27] Mindfulness is prescribed not only to treat disorders but also to promote mental health and positive living. In the United Kingdom, the National Health Service promotes mindfulness practice through programs and websites that foster healthy lifestyles.[28]

Jon Kabat-Zinn is usually credited with introducing mindfulness practice in the behavioral sciences in the 1970s. He developed the MBSR program at the University of Massachusetts Medical

School. Since that time hundreds of studies have documented the mental health benefits of mindfulness practice. It improves attention, reduces stress and anxiety, improves emotional regulation and impulse control, helps relieve chronic pain, and heightens empathy and compassion.[29] Promising research even indicates it may be as effective as medication for preventing depression relapse.[30] These concrete positive outcomes have spurred the growth of mindfulness practice in many clinical settings as a path for mental well-being.

Neuroscience

Partly as a result of evidence-based outcomes in the behavioral sciences, neuroscience is working to understand how mindfulness functions to rewire brain architecture. Brain imaging studies so far show that long-term mindfulness practice is associated with long-lasting changes in the brain, both in patterns of brain activity and in the physical structure of the brain itself. Studies at Harvard and Massachusetts General report that brain regions associated with attention, interoception, and sensory processing were actually thickened in mindfulness practitioners.[31] In another study, the amygdala, the "fight or flight" center of the brain, reduced in size after eight weeks of mindfulness practice.[32] Bestsellers, such as Daniel D. Amen's *Change Your Brain, Change Your Life,* are popularizing this research.[33] The *Harvard Business Review* article "Mindfulness Can Literally Change Your Brain," published in 2015, shows how mainstream brain science about mindfulness has become.[34]

Education

Mindfulness practice is being put to use in classrooms across the United States and beyond. Educators find it particularly effective to help children develop attention and focus skills as well as to improve emotion and impulse regulation.[35] Improved cognitive outcomes for children also drive mindfulness practice.[36] Picture first-graders pausing at the start of the school day for a full minute of mindful awareness in silence. The length of time increases as children's capacity for stillness and mindfulness grows. Slow, focused breathing and body awareness cultivate an attentiveness that children can then call upon through the prompt "just breathe," when they become emotionally overwhelmed or distressed.

Programs such as MindUp Curriculum from Scholastic, Mindful Schools (mindfulschools.org), and the Mindfulness in Schools Project (mindfulnessinschools.org) offer curriculum that applies neuroscience on mindfulness in the classroom.[37] Some educators argue that mindfulness not only is effective for children's learning but also is an effective skill for their lifelong happiness and well-being.[38]

Have you experienced mindfulness practice in a therapeutic, business, education, or sports setting? How was it introduced and explained? What were your initial reactions?

Business

In his book *Mindful Work: How Meditation Is Changing Business from the Inside Out*, Davis Gelles describes a large conference hall at General Mills with sixty or so employees entering in silence to sit restfully on cushions on the floor. The circle included men and women, employees in suits and in T-shirts, reflecting a cross section of the company. They entered in silence, closed their eyes, and began focused breathing. Mindfulness practice had begun.

Gelles goes on to recount the growing trend of mindfulness practice in the American workplace. Major companies, including
Google, General Mills, Ford Motors, Aetna, Safeway, and Patago-
nia, have introduced mindfulness in their workforces for a variety
of reasons. In some cases, executives have discovered the benefits
of mindfulness for themselves. In other cases, companies hope to
increase productivity and cut health care costs. Still others believe
it's good for business.

At the same time, employees who participate in mindfulness
practice report greater job satisfaction, lower stress levels, and improved sleep. In many companies employees can opt for mindfulness programs, much like going to the gym. Actual practices vary
from silent "mindful lunches" at Google to online mindfulness
training at Aetna. While many remain skeptical or predict a back-
lash to this trend in corporate America, it appears here to stay.[39]

Sports

Athletes are also adopting mindfulness practice to enhance
sports performance. Sports psychologists in recent decades have
offered strategies for dealing with the biggest challenges for elite
athletes: negative thoughts, performance anxiety, and lack of
focus. Professional athletes have recognized the importance of
mental training, turning to visualization, self-affirmations, and
other techniques to get athletes in "the flow," the optimal state for
sports performance. Sports organizations and athletes are turning to mindfulness-based performance enhancement (MBPE) for
performance results.

Research studies of mindfulness practice with athletes show
that mindfulness can help athletes improve mental focus, emotion regulation, body awareness, and performance.[40] In one study,

conducted by the Center for Mindfulness, at University of California, San Diego, researchers determined that mindfulness training can lead to greater focus, reduced stress, better anticipation of and recovery from internal perturbations, increased attention to bodily signals and faster neural processing, all leading to enhanced sports performance.[41] Initially developed with the US Olympic BMX Cycling team in 2014, this program is now offered widely to the sports community and beyond.[42]

Yoga

Yoga and other exercise classes remain a popular place to encounter mindfulness. Yoga in particular focuses on internal awareness of one's bodily experience. In this context mindfulness usually entails slowed breathing and scanning the body to notice sensations and feelings. It may also be accompanied by instruction on nonjudgmental awareness or acceptance.[43] Interestingly, one study reports that while people start yoga to gain flexibility and stress relief, it's the mind-body connection that keeps them coming back. This integrated spiritual framework helps them approach life with more gratitude and compassion.[44] The popularity of yoga is not only the desire for physical fitness but also the hunger for a spiritual anchor that mindfulness can cultivate.[45] The surge of yoga classes and practitioners in the last decade speaks to the concrete difference mindfulness practice can make in distracted and scattered lives.

Objections to Mindfulness

While the mindfulness movement is increasingly pervasive, it is not universally welcomed.[46] Skeptical voices raise concerns

43

about "mcmindfulness," a version of mindfulness they say both mass-produces and trivializes it. Some worry that mindfulness in the workplace is intended to keep workers compliant at best or turn them into corporate zombies at worst. A different concern expressed by some in the Buddhist community is that mindfulness is being co-opted by big business, misusing a sacred practice to increase profits rather than to reduce suffering. These voices raise serious concerns about how mindfulness practice is adapted and to what ends. On another front, some physicians express concern that the popularity of mindfulness as a one-size-fits-all will displace other, equally important health behaviors.

Do any of these objections resonate with you?
What are your concerns about mindfulness as
a Christian practice?

Adding to the pushback are secularists who fear that religion disguised as mindfulness is creeping into classrooms, boardrooms, and science labs.[47] Some Christians share these same concerns, rejecting mindfulness as a Buddhist or eastern religious practice alien to Christian faith. Some Christian parents object to mindfulness practices in their children's schools on these grounds.[48] The assumption among some Christians that mindfulness is a uniquely Buddhist practice has been surprisingly persistent, revealing a profound lack of awareness of Christian tradition.

Wrap-Up

Chapter 2 has surveyed the landscapes of Christian history and contemporary culture to discover the roots and continued resonances of mindfulness. It is the ongoing work of Christian communities and leaders to curate these resources in order to love the world in Jesus's name.

Curating mindfulness means paying attention to where and why it is taking root in many places. The rapid rise in secular mindfulness practice in the early twenty-first century means it is still a moving target, hard to pin down because it is not yet settled into institutionalized structures or regulated forms. Exploring the "where and why" can give us clues both into the hungers of the human heart and into God's reaching into human hearts and meeting people where they are, right here, right now. Faithful curating requires careful observation, using "eyes to see" and "ears to hear" how God may be at work through mindfulness in the twenty-first century as in previous centuries.

This is nothing new. Such curating is a form of mindful discernment, which has always been the work of the Christian life. We curate the culture every day seeking discernment to live faithfully as we surf the Internet choosing which sites get our attention, as we choose news sources that will shape our worldview, as we buy groceries and steward our resources. We are always making choices about how we love the world that God so loves, participating in the *missio Dei* for abundant life for all. In fact, we ignore this work at our peril. Failure to curate, to discern the spirits, and make intentional choices toward God's love for the world inevitably lead to mindless conformity to the world's values and norms.

I want to close this chapter with a note about fearing the mindfulness movement. Blind denouncements of mindfulness are as troublesome as blind acceptance. Rather than fear the mindfulness movement, we must critically curate it as we do other cultural trends. One of the most powerful witnesses Christians can make in the United States in the early twenty-first century is to live without fear. The rampant fearmongering that permeates both political and religious discourse is death-dealing, and not the way of Jesus, "There is no fear in love, but perfect love drives out fear" (1 John 4:18). This good news of fearlessness may be the most radical proclamation of good news we have!

To be clear, this is not to suggest a one-to-one correlation between mindfulness in Christian tradition and mindfulness in its current expressions in the culture. Chapter 1 makes clear that Christian mindfulness has distinctives, particularly its purpose to discover God's abundant life. Rather, I suggest that curating mindfulness in its particularly Christian forms in the tradition, as well as in its current forms in the wider culture, is the task of a faithful Christian witness that takes seriously God's presence in the world. This is what faithful Christians have always done throughout the centuries, curating Christian witness and tradition alongside the very particular cultural moment they are in, in order to live the good news of abundant life in Christ.

Chapter 3 offers concrete descriptions of the practices and postures of Christian mindfulness both for individuals and for communities.

For Further Reading

Part 1: Historical Sources

Barry, William A., SJ, *Finding God in All Things: A Companion to the Spiritual Exercises of St. Ignatius.* Notre Dame, Ind.: Ave Maria, 2009.

Brother Lawrence. *The Practice of the Presence of God.* Translated by John J. Delaney. New York: Image, 1977.

Chittester, Joan. *The Rule of Benedict: A Spirituality for the 21st Century.* 2nd ed. Spiritual Legacy Series. New York: Crossroad, 2010.

Davies, Oliver. *Celtic Spirituality.* Classics of Western Spirituality. Mahwah, N.J.: Paulist, 1999.

Hart, Columba, trans. *Hildegard of Bingen: Scivias.* Classics of Western Spirituality. Mahwah, N.J.: Paulist, 1990.

Matthewes-Green, Fredericka. *Praying the Jesus Prayer* (Ancient Spiritual Disciplines). Brewster, Mass.: Paraclete, 2011.

Meister Eckhart. *Meister Eckhart: The Essential Sermons, Commentaries, Treatises and Defense.* Classics of Western Spirituality. Translated by Edmund Colledge and Bernard McGinn. Mahwah, N.J.: Paulist, 1981.

The Sayings of the Desert Fathers. Translated by Benedicta Ward. Kalamazoo: Cistercian, 1975, rev. 1984.

Steere, Douglas V,. ed. *Quaker Spirituality: Selected Writings.* Classics of Western Spirituality. Mahwah, N.J.: Paulist, 1983.

Teresa of Avila. *The Way of Perfection.* Translated by Henry L. Carrigan (Brewster, Mass.: Paraclete Press, 2009).

Van Engen, John, trans. *Devotio Moderna: Basic Writings.* Classics of Western Spirituality. Mahwah, N.J.: Paulist, 1988.

Walsh, James, and Edmund Colledge, trans. *Julian of Norwich: Showings.* Classics of Western Spirituality. Mahwah, N.J.: Paulist, 1978.

Whaling, Frank, ed. *John and Charles Wesley: Selected Prayers, Hymns, Journal Notes, Sermons, Letters and Treatises.* Classics of Western Spirituality. Mahwah, N.J.: Paulist, 1981.

Chapter 2

Part 2: Contemporary Culture

Amen, Daniel D. *Change Your Brain, Change Your Life*. New York: Crown 1998, 2015.

Gelles, David. *Mindful Work: How Meditation Is Changing Business from the Inside Out*. Boston: Houghton Mifflin Harcourt, 2015.

Kabat-Zinn, Jon. *Wherever You Go, There You Are: Mindfulness Meditation in Everyday Life*. New York: Hyperion, 1994.

Practices and Postures of Christian Mindfulness

Basic Christian Mindfulness Practice

The starting place for Christian mindfulness practice is right here, right now. You have everything you need to get started: your breath, your body and God's presence. Read through the four steps below, then put the book down and try it.

1. Attentive Breathing

2. Attentive Embodiment

3. Acknowledgment

4. Discovery

1. Attentive Breathing (30 seconds)

First, breathe slowly and deeply. As you breathe, notice your breathing, the feel of your chest as it rises and falls, the sensation of air in your nose and lungs. Take your time to breathe in and out purposefully. Fully experience your body breathing. This first step you already do as a gift God has given you. You do not have to choose each time you take a breath. Your body chooses that for you! You *can* choose to breathe in an attentive and mindful way.

2. Attentive Embodiment (30 seconds)

What do you already know about your body awareness? Is your body a place you feel at home with God or Jesus? If this is a new idea, invite the One who made you, who knows everything about your body, and who became flesh to dwell with us, to join you in body awareness.

Continue to breathe mindfully and let your breathing fill your whole body. Visualize the oxygen filling your lungs, then your torso, then your arms and legs, providing life-giving oxygen throughout your bloodstream from the tip of your head down to your toes. Focus your attention as you continue breathing, noticing what arises in your body—sensations or feelings, perhaps a tightness here or a warm tingle there. Simple noticing is all that is required. Don't analyze, justify, or fix any of these sensations. Christians believe our bodies are blessed, consecrated by God who became flesh to dwell with us. Our en-*flesh*-ment connects us to God who meets us where we are, in our bodies, right here, right now.

3. Acknowledgment (30 seconds)

Third, acknowledge whatever arises from your mindful breathing and embodiment. Acknowledge the thoughts, feelings, sensations or attitudes that are in you right now. Whether it is positive or negative, whether you like it or don't like it, acknowledge *what is*. We spend a lot of energy every day trying to avoid, deny, repress or reject what is actually happening in our bodies. In this moment acknowledge what is there, arising in your breathing and embodiment. Some call this nonjudgmental observing. Others call it prayerful attentiveness. A common method for acknowledgment is to visualize each thing that arises as a boat floating down a river. You see it and acknowledge it is there, and let it float right on by without stopping to get on the boat or to rifle through its cargo.

To be clear, your acknowledgment does not mean that you must accept any harmful or unjust situation, only the thoughts or feelings that arise, recognizing each is there.

This step of mindfulness is an invitation to step out of the cycle of reactivity that often drives thoughts and behaviors. Not only are we prone to reactivity, but the world around us often eggs it on. Instead of reacting to what arises in our breathing and body, the step of acknowledgment allows us to see the truth of what is and hold it before God.

This is the *paying prayerful attention* part of Christian mindfulness. We pay prayerful attention to what is with an open heart to discover what God might be up to. We are open to discovery more than judgment, to listening more than speaking. As you hold all that arises before God, let God hold it with you. God is right here, right now, in your breathing and embodiment. As you acknowledge what is, also acknowledge God's sharing in it with you.

51

If you wish, visualize yourself with Jesus, together holding what you have noticed. Experience God's loving gaze upon it all in this moment.

Is the practice of simple noticing new for you?
Can you remember doing this as a child?

---

4. Discovery (30 seconds)

As you acknowledge whatever arises, holding it within God's presence, see what you discover. Do thoughts or feelings shift shapes? Increase or diminish? Does a sensation move elsewhere in your body? Does a thought or attitude disappear altogether like a boat floating away?

Again, the point here is to notice and acknowledge what you discover, not to analyze, judge, or process it. Simple noticing is the main work of mindfulness. However, noticing requires being present (steps 1 and 2) first.

Reminder

You cannot fail. There is no wrong answer. Whatever arises is what you notice and acknowledge, held simply before God. You do not have to understand, change, or act upon anything. Step into prayerful acknowledgment of *what is* right here, right now, with God.

Try It

Put the book down and walk through the four steps. As a beginner, the whole thing should take about two minutes.

It's fine if your mind wanders. Bring it back gently to the next step. After you have done this practice fifty times or so, your mind will wander less and less.

Keep Trying It

Experiment wherever you are—at a stoplight, in the elevator, shopping online—using the four steps of basic Christian mindfulness.

Practices of Christian Mindfulness

Introduction to Practices

You can stop right here and simply use the basic Christian mindfulness practice above as well as the mindful postures at the end of the chapter. However, if you want to practice existing spiritual disciplines more mindfully, keep reading. We have an embarrassment of riches in the many spiritual postures and practices we inherit from our ancient Christian family. Below is a range of spiritual practices that include mindfulness, each rooted in centuries of Christian faith and practice, adapted and simplified to help you get started.

These step-by-step instructions, often incorporating the four-step basic Christian mindfulness practice above, are intended to help beginners with a starting place. When you first learn to cook, you would probably want a recipe. The first time you go to a destination you've never been, you would probably like a map. So it is with mindfulness. The wisdom of our Christian ancestors can guide us, giving us some spiritual recipes to try. Over time, your practice will become more fluid and may not look much like these instructions at all.

✳ Warning: do not think you must do all these practices. Do not get busy "getting mindful." These are not spiritual badges to wear or spiritual duties to add to your already full to-do list. Pick one that calls to you and invite God to experiment with you in that practice for a while, at least a week. Our consumer culture has taught us to react immediately to a meal, a movie, or a pair of jeans with a "like" or "dislike." Interrupt that consumer cycle in your spiritual life, giving yourself permission to take your time to linger and explore one mindfulness practice.

Individual Practices

Breath Prayer

Description and Purpose

The breath prayer builds on the basic practice of attentive breathing. It uses what you already have—your breathing—to integrate your body, mind, and spirit in prayerful paying attention. From the very beginning, Christians have turned to breathing as prayer. In the Bible the words for "breath" and "spirit" are the same, both in Hebrew (*ruah*) and Greek (*pneuma*), revealing the deep connection between breath, spirituality, and the divine. The purpose of breath prayer is to become mindful of your life in God right here, right now, through the most basic of bodily functions: breathing.

Getting Started

1. There are many forms for breath prayer. For beginners, use step 1 of the basic Christian mindfulness practice to pay attention to your breathing (p. 49–50 above).[1] As

you take slow, deep breaths, become more aware of your breath in your body and more present to the moment.

2. Next, to focus your mindfulness on God's presence in you, say "here" as you breathe in and "now" as you breathe out. You can say the words mentally or in a soft whisper. You may also choose to use different words from Scripture or from your present need, for example, "peace," "Jesus," "Come Holy Spirit," or "spacious life."

3. Continue this breath prayer as long as you like. For beginners, I suggest eight to ten breaths.

4. To close, choose words for your final breath prayer such as "Amen," "thank you," or "let it be."

This is a simple practice for groups as well.

Mindfulness Bell

Description and Purpose

Monastic communities have punctuated the day with eight set times for prayer since the early centuries of Christianity. Called the "divine hours" or "divine offices" these fixed times for prayer were signaled by a bell so that each person would pause from work and gather with the community to pray. We can adapt this for life outside a monastery, too.

This practice is especially helpful for beginners who don't yet have an internalized rhythm for mindfulness. A mindfulness bell, using a phone app or timer, prompts regular pauses for mindfulness throughout the day. Let these be micro-invitations for you to open up space in the busyness of the day for mindful breathing and attentiveness to God.

Getting Started

1. Use a mindfulness bell phone app or automatic timer to call yourself to mindfulness practice. There are several you can download to your phone or tablet.

2. For starters, I suggest setting the bell to ring every two to three hours of your waking day. Alternately, you can set it for times that are predictably available in your schedule, for example, 7 a.m., 12 p.m., 7 p.m., 10 p.m. You know your life best, so experiment with time of day and frequency. Many find it helpful to let the bell interrupt the routine of the day to cultivate mindfulness in the midst of ongoing life.

3. When the bell rings, hear it as an invitation. Pause where you are and take sixty to ninety seconds to walk through the four steps of basic Christian mindfulness practice.

4. Note: there will be times when you are in a meeting, in a conversation, or otherwise unable to pause sixty seconds for the four steps of mindfulness. Not to worry, you have not failed and you don't have to schedule a makeup time. You can honor your mindfulness practice by simply acknowledging your desire for it. Use a silent, physical act, such as a smile or a blink of your eyes, to embody briefly and simply your desire for mindfulness.

5. Repeat the four steps the next time the mindfulness bell rings.

6. For corporate practice, your partner, friends, or church group can join together to observe the same set times using the mindfulness bell throughout the day. There is a powerful communion in knowing others are pausing, even though perhaps far away, at the same moment you are. The body of Christ mindful together.

Practicing the Presence of God

Description and Purpose

Brother Lawrence, a monk in the 1600s, found joy in his daily duties like peeling potatoes or washing dishes when he "practiced the presence of God." His purpose was, in everything he did, no matter how menial the task, to do it with God, and for the love of God. As he "practiced the presence of God," he embraced the love God had for him and for the world. This shifted his frame of reference for all daily work, no longer seeking others' approval or striving toward a goal, and instead the purpose was being with and loving God. Though he was a lowly lay brother who worked in the monastery kitchen, many sought out Brother Lawrence for his wisdom and continual peace.

While continual awareness of God has always been promoted in the Christian life—"pray without ceasing"—Brother Lawrence made it an on-the-ground practice, something we can *do* no matter what we are doing. That is, we don't have to wait until we are in church or during formal prayer, or reading the Bible, or thinking holy thoughts to "practice the presence of God." Rather, in our everyday routines, even monotony or drudgery, we can seek and claim God's life with us, right here, right now.

Getting Started

1. To begin, identify one task you do every day such as writing e-mails, preparing meals, or commuting to work.

2. Each time you do that task use the four steps of basic Christian mindfulness practice above to become aware of God's presence, right here, right now.

3. Allow God's love to fill your lungs, and then your whole body, so that you and God are doing this task together.

Scripture Mindfulness

Description and Purpose

As you spend time in Scripture, whether in Bible reading, *lectio divina*, or analytical study, mindfulness practice can help you slow down and listen to what is happening within you rather than focus on analysis alone or on figuring out a right answer. A regular mindfulness pause allows you to listen with "the ear of the heart" to the Spirit that brings Life through the Word. At any point in Scripture study or devotion, pause and turn to the four steps of mindfulness. As you notice your breathing and embodiment, acknowledge what arises as you let God hold it with you. You will discover how God is speaking to you through the Word.

Getting Started

1. As you begin your time with Scripture, you may want to set a timer to remind you to pause for mindfulness every ten minutes or so.

2. At the timer's sound, or at any point in Scripture study or devotion, pause and turn to the four steps of basic Christian mindfulness.

3. Take a moment to notice your breathing and embodiment. Acknowledge what arises.

4. Discover how God is present with you right here, right now.

5. This is also fruitful for group Bible study. After thirty minutes or so, invite the group to pause and practice the four steps of Christian mindfulness. While doing this may initially seem like an interruption in the flow of the group, you will quickly discover it can take Bible study to a deeper level through this attentive listening.

Silence

Description and Purpose

Silence is a radical, countercultural practice in our time. We are bombarded by almost-constant sound. In elevators, waiting rooms, and restaurants, music blares. In many workplaces, ear buds keep workers occupied with podcasts or music. In fact, we are so conditioned to noise that most of us are uncomfortable with silent pauses or spaces empty of sound. We may rush to fill silence in a conversation by jumping in with words or fill the empty silence of our home by turning on the TV.

Silence may be the most difficult of all prayer practices for the twenty-first-century Christian. Yet most find that once you get a taste of silence, you are hungry for more. The purpose of this practice over time is to free us from chronic overstimulation that, ironically, rather than stimulating us, actually numbs us. Silence frees us to become more sensory, aware of our lives in the present moment, and of God's abundant life offered here, now. Silence opens up space to rest, to simply breathe and be, to listen—to ourselves, to our lives, to the world around us and eventually, to God. This takes practice.

Getting Started

1. While silence may seem to be a passive act of merely eliminating noise, mindful silence actually takes a lot of intention and active practice. For beginners, decide whether you want to be still or active in your silence. For some, stillness is so distracting that it's better to start with movement as you explore silence. You know your temperament, and either way is fine.

2. For those who want to be active, select an activity you already do regularly alone, such as walking, for your experiment with silence. For those who want to be still, select a private place where you know you won't be disturbed.

3. Because beginners often get overwhelmed at the thought of long stretches of silence, start with four to five minutes of silence. Set a timer if you wish. As your thoughts wander, which they will, let each thought float on by like a cloud, and gently return your focus to your breathing through your body.

4. As you sit in stillness, or move in your activity, begin the first step of mindfulness by breathing deeply and attentively. Focus your thoughts on your breath and its movement through your body. Continue to breathe deeply and slowly. Settle in to your breathing and your body in the silence.

5. Next, shift your focus from your breathing to your body and the thoughts, feelings, or sensations that now arise. Notice the silence and the sounds that you hear within it. Continue steps 2, 3, and 4 of the basic Christian mindfulness practice.

6. For corporate practice, follow these steps together. Group silence can be very supportive and powerful. For beginners, group silence is an especially helpful jumpstart.

Prayer of St. Patrick

Description and Purpose

The traditional "breastplate prayer" of Patrick (fifth century) offers many petitions in its entirety. The most well-known stanza describes the three-dimensional space our bodies occupy—above, below, in front, behind, on my left and right—and claims Christ in each. We use this portion of Patrick's prayer here to make us mindful of our embodiment and of Christ's presence with our embodiment.

Getting Started

1. Begin step 1 of mindfulness practice with focused breathing.

2. After six to eight slow breaths, turn to step 2 of mindfulness practice: attentive embodiment.

3. During step 2, use this portion of the breastplate prayer. With each phrase of the prayer, focus your attention on that aspect of your body the phrase describes. For example, during the phrase "Christ before me," focus your awareness on the front of your body and Christ's presence there. Experience Christ present in each dimension of your embodiment throughout the prayer.

> Christ with me, Christ before me, Christ behind me,
>
> Christ within me, Christ beneath me, Christ above me,
>
> Christ to right of me, Christ to left of me,
>
> Christ in my lying, Christ in my sitting, Christ in
> my rising,
>
> Christ in the heart of all who think of me,
>
> Christ on the tongue of all who speak to me,
>
> Christ in the eye of all who see me,
>
> Christ in the ear of all who hear me.[2]

61

4. Continue to step 3, acknowledging what arises.

5. Finish with step 4, mindful of discovering Christ's presence.

Daily Examen

Description and Purpose

The Examen is not an exam or test to see if we've been good, as the name might suggest. Rather, it examines the day to look for traces of God at work. The daily Examen is way of learning to see God in our everyday lives. Throughout each day we move closer to and further from God. The purpose of the Examen is to become more keenly aware of this movement toward and away from God so that we more frequently cooperate with what God is doing in us and in the world. The Examen offers a daily practice that sharpens our mindfulness of God so that we come to *expect* to see what God is up to, the *missio Dei*.

Getting Started

1. Select a ten-minute window of time in which you can review the day, perhaps either at the end of the day or the next morning to look back over the previous day.

2. During that ten minutes, sit in a place that allows you uninterrupted time to reflect. You may want to bring a journal.

3. Begin with step 1 from the mindfulness practice above. Focus attentively on your breathing, first in your nose and lungs and then in your whole-body breathing. Use several deep breaths to settle into the present moment, here, now.

4. Next, turn your attention to the events of the day. What stands out as you review the day? What gets your attention? The goal here is not to exhaustively list everything that happened, but rather to pay attention to what arises in your noticing. You may notice specific events, for example, a doctor's appointment or a conversation at work. Or you may notice feelings that arose in the day, for example, anxiety or frustration. Spend a couple of minutes just reviewing the day and noticing what arises.

5. Next, walk through these questions for reflection.[3] For beginners, I suggest you keep it simple and use one or two of the guiding questions as you begin to pay attention to your day. Give yourself five minutes or so to reflect, using a journal to write your reflections if that helps you focus.

   • When did I feel the most life-giving energy?

   • When did I feel despair, anger, meanness, or a sense of being drained?

   • When did I feel God's presence or God's absence, or feel close or far from God?

6. Finally, ask

   • from this review, how is God calling me forward into the next day? or

   • what does God want me to notice and who is God calling me to be?

   Spend several minutes here, again journaling your reflections if that helps you stay focused.

7. Close by returning awareness to your breathing and give thanks.

Prayer of Recollection

Description and Purpose

The prayer of recollection emerges from the work of Teresa of Avila during the sixteenth century, a time of great flowering for Christian spirituality.[4] The purpose of this simple approach is to "recollect," or remind us that God dwells with each of us right here, right now. She calls this being mindful of "this little heaven of my soul." Teresa advises using this prayer anywhere anytime to recall and rest in God's presence:

> Give me the grace to recollect myself in the little heaven of my soul where You have established Your dwelling. There You let me find You, there I feel that You are closer to me than anywhere else, and there You prepare my soul quickly to enter into intimacy with You.... Help me O Lord, to withdraw my senses from exterior things, make them docile to the commands of my will, so that when I want to converse with You, they will retire at once, like bees shutting themselves up in the hive in order to make honey.[5]

This prayer reclaims our distracted senses so that we can mindfully "converse with You." John of the Cross, Thomas Merton, and others have developed several methods for the prayer of recollection.

Getting Started

1. Begin with step 1 of basic Christian mindfulness, focused breathing.

2. As you turn to step 2, begin Teresa's prayer of recollection. With each phrase, notice the ways your embodiment is "the little heaven of my soul where You have established

Your dwelling." Let each phrase help gather your senses and awareness of this present moment.

3. Continue to step 3, acknowledgment of what arises as you hold this with God.

4. Finish with step 4, paying attention as you discover this present moment with God's abundant life.

Welcoming Prayer

Description and Purpose

The Welcoming Prayer is a more recent practice that uses mindfulness to focus and welcome one's current experience—no matter what it is—in order to surrender all of it to God. The deep wisdom here is that trying to banish difficult feelings and thoughts only gives them more power to take root and grow. Anyone who has tried to meditate has experienced this: the more you try *not* to think about something, the more it dominates your thoughts.

Instead, the purpose here is to acknowledge and welcome existing feelings, which has the surprising result of reducing their power and dominance. Welcoming what is, in fact, already happening inside you disarms anxiety, anger, fear, or frustration with amazing effect. Suppression serves to concentrate the feelings, giving them more subtle and intense power.

To be clear, the purpose of this practice is not to welcome feelings in order to wallow in them or obsess over them. Nor is the purpose to justify and bolster feelings. Rather, the purpose is to honestly acknowledge and welcome what we experience *right now*. Only then can our eyes be opened to what is truly there, including God's active presence. With "eyes to see" we can welcome and receive what is already there in order to then surrender it to God. This takes practice.

Getting Started

1. Begin with step 1 of basic Christian mindfulness practice. Focus mindfully on your breathing as your breath fills your lungs and then your whole body.

2. Next, begin step 2, attending to your body. Become aware of sensations as well as emotions right now. Take time to be fully present to your breathing and to your body.

3. Next, move to step 3, allowing yourself to fully feel and name whatever thoughts, feelings, or sensations that arise. Acknowledge what is without judgment. It may be anxiety, fear, frustration, scatteredness, pride, or obsessive thoughts.

4. Notice the feeling that seems to have the most energy and welcome it. Just as you would respond to a guest knocking on the door, open the door and welcome the feeling in. Visualize yourself opening the door and receiving the feeling as a guest. Alternately, you can visualize the feeling as an infant that you hold and cradle in your arms. Spend a minute or so visualizing this. As you welcome the feeling, you also welcome God's presence in this moment, right here, right now. Note: This step is especially critical because without mindful welcome, our impulse is to suppress difficult feelings, thus giving them more subtle and intense power.

5. Note that this practice is not asking you to accept an unjust situation, but only the feelings that emerge in you.

6. Finally, surrender the thought or feeling into God's keeping. This is the most radical and difficult step of all. We often find that we are actually strongly attached to the very feelings we want to suppress. Sometimes difficult feelings serve some secondary benefit, of which we are not aware until we try to let them go. For example, it can be disconcerting to realize that our anger fuels a sense of self-righteousness that makes us feel pretty good. We don't want to surrender our anger and thereby lose our status of one-upmanship! Father Thomas Keating and others have developed a prayer specifically for this step, and it shows up in different versions. Use this prayer and let it sink into your bones:

> I let go of my desire for security and survival.
>
> I let go of my desire for esteem and affection.
>
> I let go of my desire for power and control.
>
> I let go of my desire to change the feeling or situation.
>
> God, I give you my_____.

Great Commandment Mindfulness

Description and Purpose

This mindfulness practice uses Jesus's Great Commandment in Matthew, "'You must love the Lord your God with all your heart, with all your being, and with all your mind.' This is the first and greatest commandment. And the second is like it: 'You must love your neighbor as you love yourself'" (Matt 22:37-39). The purpose of great commandment mindfulness is to focus our prayerful attention on God's love for us and our response. We begin by being present to God's love with us and allowing that divine love to carry our love outward to neighbor and world. This method can be especially powerful when used during online activity as a sort of digital *shema*.

Getting Started

1. Begin with step 1 of mindful breathing for a moment, at least thirty seconds. Allow yourself to be present to your breath in your nose, lungs, and whole body in slow, deep breaths.

2. Turn to step 2 of embodiment, becoming aware of the thoughts, feelings, and sensations that arise in your body. Notice which limbs or locations are involved.

3. As you move into step 3, acknowledge whatever arises and hold it with God, letting God's presence become more and more real to you in this moment. Feel God's loving gaze upon you, God's own child. Be present with God's love.

4. Now, dwelling in God's loving gaze, hear Jesus's words, "You must love the Lord your God with all your heart, with all your being, and with all your mind.... You must love your neighbor as you love yourself" (Matt 22:37-39). Notice in this present moment how you are opening to this love for God, neighbor, and self, right here, right now. Is it located somewhere particular in your body? What are you aware of?

5. Let yourself sink deeply down into this love, God's love for you coming full circle in your love for God, neighbor, and self. Imagine this love in you now with roots sinking down into the earth. Visualize the buds springing forth in your heart.

6. If you find you cannot experience love for God, neighbor, or self, then return to step 3 above, and rest in God's love. You don't have to force yourself to love or figure out why you can't. Simply surrender to God's love for you, neighbor, and world. Let God carry this for you right now.

7. Close with gratitude for whatever you experience.

8. For corporate experience, use loving mindfulness practice as guided meditation in a group.

Which practices speak to your desire for a more mindful Christian life? Notice which ones you'd like to try.

Jesus Prayer

Description and Purpose

The Jesus Prayer is an ancient prayer that originates in early desert Christianity. While it has been especially cherished by Orthodox Christians over the centuries, the Jesus Prayer is widely practiced among Christians of all traditions. Its simplest form, "Lord Jesus Christ, Son of God, have mercy on me," has been adapted for different times and places. The purpose of the Jesus Prayer is its focus on mercy in this present moment, especially when mindfulness reveals anxiety, confusion, or fear.

Getting Started

1. Using steps 1 and 2 of the basic Christian mindfulness practice above, become mindful of your breathing, the breath in your nose, lungs, and body. Become present

to your body in this moment, noticing the feelings, thoughts, or sensations that arise as you breathe slowly and deeply. Be present in your breath and body, right here, right now.

2. When you are ready, begin the Jesus Prayer, in its traditional form or with your own adapted words, for example, "Lord Jesus Christ, Son of God, have mercy on me/ us," "Jesus, wrap me in your mercy now," or "Holy Spirit, let your mercy cover me."

3. Next, move into step 3 of basic practice, acknowledge and let God hold with you whatever arises. In this step, you acknowledge *whatever is* as your real life right now held within God's Life. Become aware of God's presence with you and in you right here, right now.

4. As you chant it softly, let the repetitions form a rhythm with your breathing. With each inhalation, draw in divine mercy, letting it flow through you and, with exhalation, letting the mercy flow out into the world that God so loves.

5. Close with gratitude.

6. For corporate practice, this method can be used as guided prayer with groups.

Communal Practices

While many of the practices above can be done corporately as well as individually, there are some Christian practices that are almost always done communally. Offered here are several common practices that can incorporate Christian mindfulness, though this list is certainly not exhaustive.

Holy/Mindful Conversation

Description and Purpose

Through Christian history, human conversation has been identified as a key context for spiritual growth, a place of truth-telling where God can speak into our lives. We are lucky if we have one or two good friends who speak truth into our lives, tell us things we don't always want to hear, and listen to us with the "ear of the heart." It's not only good friends, however, who offer us such holy conversation. It may be mentors, family members, healers, or coworkers. Occasionally, we may even find ourselves in holy conversation with strangers.

John Wesley, even in the 1700s, was concerned about super-ficial conversation that flitted over the surface of life without deep listening or authentic speech. He advises, for both private conversation and more public Christian conferencing, that if we seek authentic relationships with God and others, we must take conversation seriously and proceed mindfully because God is at work there.[6]

Remember it is not we, but God, who makes conversation holy. We practice holy conversation as we listen deeply and speak truly. We drop the masks that we present to the world and to God. Holy conversation listens, not to surface words alone, but to the depth notes underneath, the longing expressed, the silence in what is not said, the dawning awareness that God is up to something. In the work of having eyes to see and ears to hear God's abundant life right here, right now, we need one another's help. The way that leads to abundant life is traveled by all of us together.

Getting Started

1. For our purposes here, we will focus on holy conversation between two people, not on its practice in larger, public

71

settings. Remember that your own, individual mindfulness practice will enhance your ability to be present and mindful in conversations with others.

2. First, become aware of God's presence in the conversation. This may take the form of a silent prayer inviting God to join you, or an internal acknowledgment that God was here first.

3. Aware of God's guiding presence, use two or three attentive breaths to let go of your own need to control, be right, or solve a problem. The goal is to listen for God, both in yourself and in the other person, with "the ear of the heart," not trying to fix, analyze, or advise.

4. Notice how hard this is! It is very difficult because the world tells us that helping means fixing people's problems. The world wants to avoid pain and see immediate results. Instead, exercise the open, patient listening to God that is usually required for true healing and transformation.

5. As you speak and listen, use step 3 of the mindfulness practice to acknowledge what arises from the heart without evaluating or judging it. Hold it with God, paying prayerful attention, allowing God's loving gaze to dwell in your conversation.

6. Use these or similar questions to help you listen to the depths spoken:

   • What is the longing (or hope or tug) underneath the words?

   • What is my/your prayer for this?

   • What do we hear in the silence?

   • Where is God's voice in this?

7. Sometimes, the most powerful holy conversation has few words and much silence, or tears.

8. At the end of the conversation, either singly or jointly, notice any insights God has revealed during this time and give thanks. Noticing discoveries helps them become planted in you.

Spiritual Direction

Description and Purpose

Spiritual direction provides a more formal and structured practice of holy conversation. A spiritual director is a companion and guide who commits to deep listening for God in the life and words of the directee. The purpose of regular meetings over time is for both the spiritual director and the directee to pay prayerful attention to God's call and movement so that the directee can cooperate and participate in God's abundant life. Journeying together allows for clearer "eyes to see" and "ears to hear" the reign of God right here, right now, in the directee's life.

Spiritual direction is not psychotherapy or life coaching. Spiritual directors do not give direction in the sense of advice, fixing, or problem-solving. Rather, the directing they do is to direct attention to where and how God is speaking in the everyday life of the directee. Spiritual direction provides consistent practice in being present to one's own life in order to hear God's desires spoken in the heart. The more one sits with a spiritual director, the more one becomes aware of God's presence throughout the day, in all of life. It cultivates greater God-mindfulness.

Chapter 3

Getting Started

1. First, ask yourself whether spiritual direction is right for you at this time in your life. The professional guild of spiritual directors, Spiritual Directors International (SDI), has tools on its website for you to explore the question of readiness (SDIWorld.org).

2. To find a spiritual director, first talk to people you know. Ask if they have a spiritual director or can recommend one. Also check with your church, pastor, or counselor for referrals. Other resources include retreat centers, theology schools, and spiritual direction training programs.

3. Spiritual Directors International also provides a listing of SDI members. You can use their online tool to locate spiritual directors in your area.

4. Once you identify a spiritual director, take time in your first visit to discern whether this is a good fit for you. Not all spiritual directors are suitable for all people. Be candid about your questions or concerns, and see if it feels right. The Spiritual Directors International website offers questions to ask a prospective spiritual director.

Mindful Hospitality

Description and Purpose

Christian hospitality is more than entertaining family and friends. It is welcoming the stranger as Christ, a renewed spiritual discipline as we move into a more interfaith, intercultural world. Extending welcome to the "other" is a form of Christian witness, following Jesus's call, "I was a stranger and you welcomed me" (Matt 25:35). However, when we are not mindful in our welcome

74

of others, we can do harm. When we don't *pay prayerful atten-tion in the present moment to God's abundant life*, right here, right now, then we too often expect the "other" to conform to our own norms and expectations. We can mindlessly disregard the particu-lar characteristics, history, and gifts the stranger brings when it may be in those very particulars that God is most profoundly at work. We must let the stranger be strange, so that we can welcome Jesus in the other, and discover what God is up to, right here, right now.

Without mindful hospitality, we are likely to focus on how we can be fantastic hosts rather than focusing on how God might show up in the stranger. This shifts our focus of awareness from ourselves to God, and frees us from the perfectionistic pressures that too often accompany efforts to welcome. Mindfulness prac-tice below is suggested for hosts extending hospitality and can be done at any time before, during, and after extending welcome.

Getting Started

1. Start by inviting those hosting to use the four-step method of mindfulness together as an intentional prayer practice before you begin any welcoming activity. Decide whether you will lead them through the four steps silently or invite verbal sharing in steps 3 and 4. This preparation can transform their welcome.

2. Begin step 1 with focused breathing, taking time for eight to ten slow breaths to turn awareness away from the preparations for welcome, to breathing.

3. Lead the group to step 2, embodiment. Invite each person to scan his or her own body, attentive to each person's current physical experience in this moment.

75

4. As you move from step 2 to step 3, invite everyone to pay attention especially to the longing of their hearts that has prompted the group to extend this welcome. Hold these with God in step 3 and pay attention to discoveries in step 4.

5. Use this mindfulness practice again when the hospitality activity has ended as a way to be present and reflect. Hosts may find they are frustrated, disappointed, or exhilarated. Pay attention to breathing and embodiment, and hold within God's loving gaze whatever arises.

6. Using a mindfulness practice as part of hospitality will help hosts as well as guests become more aware of how God's abundant life is present right here, right now.

Mindful Social Action

Description and Purpose

Active engagement in social justice is critical for Christian witness if we love the world that God created and loves. The purpose of mindfulness in social action is to stay rooted in the *missio Dei* so that we participate in what God is doing in the world. Mindfulness can wake us up when we get busy with our own agenda or promote our ego-investment in being right. In addressing systemic injustice, we can fall prey to the cycle of reactivity that breeds fear and mistrust and reduces the "other" to a caricature. Mindfulness helps us to be honest about our motives and courageous about our desires. Mindful social action keeps our eye on God's outpouring and leading, on God's shalom to sustain us in the long arc of the journey to justice.[7]

Mindfulness is especially important if we want to sustain social commitments over the long haul. It's easy to get burned out if we carry everything on our shoulders and leave God behind. Our own passion for justice can make us vulnerable to self-righteousness, belittling those with whom we disagree or even mirroring the very behaviors we find offensive. As Christians, our holy anger is a charism to be treasured and stewarded through nonviolent action. Exercised mindfully, our longing for God's reign to "let justice roll down like waters, and righteousness like an ever-flowing stream" (Amos 5:24) can bear real fruit in the world. Mindfulness practice below is suggested for leaders of social action events such as a rally, march, legislative action, canvassing, or organizing. This practice can be done at any time before, during, and after events.

Getting Started

1. Use the four-step method of basic Christian mindfulness with the leadership team as an intentional prayer practice before an event. Decide whether you will lead them through the four steps silently or invite verbal sharing in steps 3 and 4. This preparation can be transforming not only for the leadership team but also the entire event.

2. Begin step 1 with focused breathing, taking time for eight to ten slow breaths to turn awareness away from event preparations to breathing.

3. Lead the group to step 2, embodiment. Invite each person to scan his or her own body, attentive to each person's current physical experience in this moment.

4. As you move from step 2 to step 3, invite everyone to pay attention especially to the longing of their hearts that emboldens the group to action. Hold these with God in step 3 and pay attention to discoveries in step 4.

5. Use this mindfulness practice again after the event as a way to be present and reflect. People may find they are frustrated, disappointed, or exhilarated. Pay attention to breathing and embodiment, and hold within God's loving gaze whatever arises.

6. Use mindfulness practice to ground social action in God's abundant life right here, right now. When practiced over time, individuals in the group will be more and more able to stay present to themselves, others, and God.

Mindfulness in Corporate Worship

Description and Purpose

Perhaps the most common corporate Christian practice is weekly worship. God's people gather to praise, lament, and proclaim the good news together. Perhaps because it is so familiar, worship often becomes a place of rote religion, where we go through the motions but have no idea why. We may become numbed by routines of worship that keep us comfortable and complacent. Conversely, we may become hypercritical consumers, expressing preferences for sermon topics or screen graphics. When we are not mindful, we can easily focus on surface satisfaction—"what do I get out of it?"—rather than honest encounter with the One who made all things visible and invisible.

Mindfulness wakes us up, requiring us to be present with God right here, right now, aware of our breathing and our bodies in this place of worship, at this moment. Even within our Sunday morning routines, simple mindfulness can enliven and transform worship. As we become more mindful in worship, we bring our whole, real selves, giving witness in worship to how we discover and live God's abundant life.

Getting Started

1. First, if you think of your church's worship service as a weekly event you attend or observe, begin to shift your frame of reference. Worship is not like a movie or concert where we come to watch the show. If you have been a longtime churchgoer, depending on your tradition, just walking into a sanctuary may trigger the passive observation mode in your brain. Instead, think of yourself as an active participant, necessary to the worship service. Your presence and participation matter to God and matter to the gathered body of Christ.

2. Prepare yourself on the way to church or in the opening moments of worship to be present and mindful in corporate worship. As you drive or sit, focus on steps 1 and 2 of mindfulness practice, breathing deeply and slowly, aware of your breath in your nose and lungs, and then becoming aware of your body. This focus on the present moment keeps you awake so that you can pay prayerful attention.

3. Step 3 can be especially revealing as you approach worship. Acknowledge whatever arises in you and hold it with God for a moment. Let the rest of the worship be a playground of discovery as you hear what God has to say to you today and as you give voice through worship, hymns, prayers, Scriptures, and sacraments. Worship both informs and calls upon your witness and discipleship. Your voice contributes to this testimony.

4. As another aid to mindfulness, look over the bulletin and identify one or two times in the service you will return to the first two steps of breathing and body awareness. Mark them in the bulletin as reminders.

5. For corporate practice, invite others with you on the way to church or sitting together as worship begins to pause and breathe slowly and deeply, doing the first two steps of mindfulness together. Encourage children to notice sounds, sights, smells, and their own bodies.

Postures for Christian Mindfulness: Daily Life Prompts

It's easy to compartmentalize spirituality into boxes labeled "church," "Bible," or "prayer." Mindfulness practice allows us to pay prayerful attention to our lives in God with every breath, in any moment, in any place. Christian mindfulness does not require formal prayer practices. It can grow organically in mundane places of your everyday life. You can cultivate awareness of your life within God's abundant life throughout your day so that you live your life close to the heartbeat of God. Such mindful living blesses you and the world. The last chapter will talk more about this.

To incorporate mindfulness into common daily activities, keep it simple. Introduce the four steps of Christian mindfulness practice into any activity of the day. Alternately, begin with only step 1, adding attentive breathing to your daily routine. Below are prompts to help you become more mindful of your life with God through the day. Play around with some of these and imagine the shape Christian mindfulness might take in your daily life.

Waking and Sleeping

Upon opening your eyes in the morning or upon going to bed, incorporate any or all steps of the mindfulness practice to become aware of God right here, right now. If you become aware of particular anxieties about the day or night ahead, notice these and hold them in God's loving presence.

Eating and Drinking

There is an increasing literature on mindful eating, a way of being present both to our bodies and to food. Use breathing and body mindfulness to notice your hunger and satiation, physical sensations we often aren't aware of. When we are not mindful, we are prone to excess in both eating and drinking. With greater awareness of each bite or drink, you may find your gratitude increases for all the sustenance God provides. It's no surprise that so much of Jesus's ministry occurs within table fellowship, including our central Christian practice, the Lord's Supper. When we connect Jesus's table fellowship with our own, we see our eating and drinking afresh as a holy gift. Pause for mindful blessing before all food and drink. Take a moment to hold all your sensations, this food and drink, within God's presence, right here, right now.

Children and Mindfulness

Children often adopt mindfulness practice naturally and quickly. They tend to be more body aware and become curious when invited to pay attention to breathing and embodiment. Here are a few suggestions for adapting the four steps for the children in your life, though you will know best what will be helpful to them.

1. Ritualize the practice through regular associations with concrete objects or places: a car seat, a mindfulness mat, a candle, or a bell a child can regularly use.

2. Start with step 2, noticing our bodies, and allow the child to identify sensations and feelings she or he notices. Then move to attentive breathing of step 1. Invite the child to place her or his hand on her or his tummy to feel the breath go in and out.

3. Engage the child's imagination in step 3 as Jesus joins her or him right here, right now, with the child in this moment. Most can easily visualize God's presence.

4. Give children a chance to share out loud what they discover, while being open to their giggles, wonder, complaints, or questions.

Driving, Biking, Riding, Walking

We spend much of each day going from one place to another, transported by car, bus, bike, rail, or on foot. Whether commuting to work or taking kids to school, being "on the way" for so much of our day is a liminal, in-between space, a wonderful invitation to Christian mindfulness. This in-between is the paradigmatic pilgrim way of the entire Christian life, making us aware of God's reign inbreaking already and, at the same time, of the not-yet fulfillment of God's new creation. Invite God to join you in whatever journeying you make each day, incorporating mindfulness practice "on the way."

Buying and Consuming

Our purchasing habits may be the most unconsciously driven of all our daily activities. From highway billboards to computer pop-up ads to podcast sponsors to Facebook feeds, we are bombarded by commercial messages aimed at multiple levels of consciousness, all intended to motivate us to buy and consume. We are sold fantasies of being richer, thinner, prettier, healthier, and happier with the implicit message that whoever you are and whatever your life, it is not enough. As Christians, we witness to the One who brings abundant life. Before you walk into Wal-Mart or fill your cart on Amazon, give yourself thirty seconds to breathe attentively; notice thoughts, feelings, and sensations that arise in your body; and pay prayerful attention to Jesus with you right here, right now. You may be surprised at what you discover.

Which daily life prompt speaks to your desire for a more mindful Christian life? Notice which ones you'd like to try.

Working and Playing

Studies suggest that Americans work more hours than ever before. Work-life balance continues to be a struggle for most, and is a primary value for the generation now entering the workforce. Mindfulness practice won't change the demands of work but will change the way you deal with them. If you want "eyes to see" and "ears to hear" the kingdom of God, even when you are at work, experiment with mindfulness practice at regular times in your workday, before you go into meetings, or after particularly difficult tasks. Invite others to join you. Even forms of play can become as mindlessly numbing as work if we are not intentional. If our playtime is given to overstimulation, particularly with screen time, we can find ourselves drained rather than refreshed, our energy dulled rather than creatively engaged. Use breathing and embodiment practice to notice how play energizes you.

Chapter 3

Talking, Texting, and Posting

Whether in person, on the phone, in e-mail, or while messaging or posting online, we have opportunities each day for mindful communication. This may be one of our greatest opportunities for radical Christian witness in a world where reactive speech gets rewarded. Mindfulness practice can interrupt whatever mental mixtapes are playing in your head as you anticipate what you will say next instead of listening deeply to what the other person is saying. When communicating online we must be careful not to leave our Christian identity behind at the login screen. To break the cycle of reactivity that accompanies so much talking, texting, and posting, turn to attentive breathing and body awareness to be present in this moment, present to those with whom you are communicating, and present to yourself. This mindfulness helps you to then see God in this moment, in this interaction, right here, right now. The person in front of me (or at the other end of my text) is a child of God, also held in God's loving heart. Christian witness is awake to God's reign at hand. Here are a few strategies for taking time to be present in communication:

1. When you find yourself carried away by your own or another's emotions, whether online or face-to-face, utilize your own pause button, "Wow, that's a lot for me to take in. Let me catch my breath for a minute and consider it." Use this pause for attentive breathing and embodiment to become present and notice what is arising.

2. It's very important for Christians to exercise nonviolent communication by not participating in online speech, texting, or e-mail that escalates to dominate and win at all costs. Use the simple phrase, "This conversation is

84

too important to have online (or by text or e-mail). Let's talk."

3. Also, many principles of holy conversation (above) can guide our mindful talking, texting, and posting.

Pets and Mindfulness

Animals can be great partners in mindfulness. In fact, sometimes our pets are our best teachers of mindfulness because animals tend to be present wherever they are, fully themselves as created by God. A dog does not try to be a tree or a chair. It is willing and wholehearted in its creatureliness. Let the animals in your life call you to simple presence, to attentive breathing in your own body and life. As you watch them breathe and move, let their model teach you how to be present with God, right here, right now.

Conclusion

There are many ways to practice Christian mindfulness. The best way is the one that works for you. Be patient and gentle with yourself, willing to experiment and explore. The Lord of Life, as close as your own breath, as constant as your heartbeat, will meet you where you are here and now.

For Further Reading

Finley, James. *Christian Meditation: Experiencing the Presence of God.* New York: HarperCollins, 2004.

Merton, Thomas. *Contemplative Prayer*, reissue. New York: Image, 1971.

Owens, L. Roger. *What We Need Is Here: Practicing the Heart of Christian Spirituality.* Nashville: Upper Room, 2015.

Rohr, Richard. *The Naked Now.* New York: Crossroad, 2009.

Thompson, Marjorie J. *Soul Feast: An Invitation to the Christian Spiritual Life,* rev. ed. Louisville: Westminster John Knox, 2014.

Vennard, Jane E. *Truly Awake, Fully Alive: Spiritual Practices to Nurture Your Soul.* Nashville: SkyLight Paths, 2013.

Wolpert, Daniel. *Creating a Life with God: The Call of Ancient Prayer Practices.* Nashville: Upper Room, 2003.

Chapter 4

Christian Mindfulness Today

Here and Now

W hat are you waiting for? There is no other time and no other place that is more holy or spiritual than here, now. The surprisingly radical claim of the Christian life is that God is at work right here, right now, no matter where you are or what you are doing. This simple and outrageous notion challenges all of our assumptions about where God shows up. Christians can unwittingly promote the idea that God only shows up at church or in the Bible or in prayer. Especially troublesome is the prevalent view that God sits on a cloud somewhere watching it all from afar, occasionally mildly amused, but mostly mad. These images and assumptions suggest that God actively withholds divine presence until we have jumped through some hoop. This is in precise contradiction to the very message Jesus proclaimed, "The reign of God is at hand!" God's abundant life is present now!

What are you waiting for? What gets in the way of you experiencing God's presence now?

This good news blows open the categories of "religious" and "spiritual." We don't have to wait until we are sitting in church to experience God's abundant life in us. We don't have to achieve some level of biblical proficiency or prove we are worthy in prayer first, to experience this present life held by God. This is available to us with each breath. Yet we will miss it if we don't pay attention, if we are not mindful in the present. The practice of Christian mindfulness is a simple starting place to connect to abundant life rooted in the sacred, spacious, dynamic life of God.

Mindfulness as Countercultural Christian Witness

Mindfulness practice is itself one way Christians can proclaim good news in our time. We make a countercultural witness when we live a free, real, rooted, grateful, and openhearted life. More than ever our world needs to hear this good news of God's abundant life. Each time we pause to rest mindfully in God's presence or draw our attention to our breathing or give our full attention to the persons we are talking to, we are practicing this good news. For Christians, then, mindfulness practice is not just the latest self-help fad or merely a nice thing to do for ourselves, but a form of Christian witness in the world. Christian mindfulness gives witness to abundant life in the way of Jesus, a life awake to the reign of God here, now, and to come.

This book began with a description of daily life, disconnected from deep roots and driven by multitasking and digital distractedness. This description will sound familiar to most. The speed of life increases as microprocessing capacity increases, like a runaway train as the world goes by in a blur with no time to get our bearings and no way to brake. Our brains struggle to absorb and process the assault of sensory inputs. As a culture, we have not developed social infrastructures or strategies to help humans keep up with the technological advances we impulsively adopt.[1] To be sure, technology is not the enemy. Rather, our mindless conforming to whatever hits our cerebral cortex first—an image or text or sound—is what holds us captive.

Perhaps never before in human history has the practice of Christian mindfulness been more critical or more life-giving. This particular historical moment cries out for spiritual practices that point to the holy in our midst, that call us to the sacred center that holds our lives, that remind us who we really are as beloved by God, that empower our lives with nourishing roots. Christian tradition is full of such spiritual practices and mindfulness is one of them.

Who in your life needs this good news right now? Take a moment to hold those you love, and yourself, in this question and pay attention to who or what arises.

Making a Difference in the World

Christian mindfulness is not merely a private act between God and me. Like all spiritual practices, it will make a real difference in the world. Christian mindfulness of God is a charism enacted in lives poured out for the world, in imitation of Jesus's own self-giving for us. Jesus says that his disciples will be known, not as super meditation gurus or as theological warriors, but because "This is how everyone will know that you are my disciples, when you love each other" (John 13:35). Jesus's love is not an ethereal ideal or a gushy feeling, but an on-the-ground love, lived out concretely with neighbors near and far; a love visible enough for others to see in the ways we live and act.

Mindfulness keeps us wide awake on the Jesus path that leads us into the world God so loves. The *missio Dei* is made plain in Jesus's mission, spelled out in Luke 4:18-19, *"to preach good news to the poor, to proclaim release to the prisoners and recovery of sight to the blind, to liberate the oppressed, and to proclaim the year of the Lord's favor."* It's hard to imagine a stronger statement of making a difference: captives freed, blind recovering sight. When we follow Jesus we participate in God's mission, God's dream for the world.

Without practices to keep us attentive, the blur of frenzied lives and consumerism can numb us to the inequality and suffering around us. To make matters worse, these same forces keep us feeling powerless to act. Following Jesus means staying awake to the ways we participate in unjust systems so that we can instead turn our attention to God's transforming mission in the world. Gospel mindfulness turns our lives toward love, justice, and mercy. If mindfulness is not leading us to act in the world with greater clarity toward God's shalom, we must reexamine our practice and its foundations.

Christian mindfulness not only challenges us to make a difference for systemic injustice in the world, it also roots us as we do so. Chapter 3 offers suggestions for mindfulness practice in the context of social activism. The work of justice requires deep spiritual roots to sustain us amid the winds of disappointments and setbacks. Regular mindfulness practice helps peacemakers keep our eyes and ears on God when we are tempted to throw up our hands in resignation or respond with disdain to those who reject reconciliation. We must be mindful to remember Who is redeeming the world when we are tempted to believe it is we ourselves.

What difference do you hope to make in your life, in your community, in the world, through Christian mindfulness? Hold these longings mindfully with God.

Christian mindfulness also makes a difference for the world in routine, daily life. These differences may seem small and insignificant, yet Jesus often describes the kingdom of God through small things like a mustard seed and yeast (Matt 13). The marks of Christian mindfulness (being free, real, rooted, grateful, and openhearted) are enacted through daily encounters with others. These small acts of humble clarity open up space to breathe, the way yeast creates airy space in dough, leavening the world in ways we cannot see or may never know. Perhaps I am more able to offer compassion instead of frustration to someone taking my time. Perhaps I offer understanding instead of judgment to a young person angry at the world. Such spacious moments offer glimpses of the kingdom of God among us, a life of good news.

Interfaith Connections

In our interfaith, interreligious world, mindfulness practice can be one meeting place with our neighbors. Increasingly, we have friends, coworkers, neighbors, and family members of different faiths and no faith, all of them beloved by God. Christians can meet Buddhists, as well as other religious and nonreligious practitioners of mindfulness, in this shared practice.

Through work and school, and as we work together for the good of our communities, people of different faiths are discovering one another. It can be easier to connect first through a shared activity than through belief systems as a starting place. We don't have to wait until we can fully grasp another's entire religion before we can reach out in friendship. In fact, Jesus offers us the model of this: not once in the Gospels does Jesus evaluate or test a person's beliefs before he heals them or feeds them. He never asks, "Do you believe in the God of Abraham, Isaac, and Jacob?" or "Are you observing the Torah commandments?" as a precondition of his preaching or healing. He simply reaches out.

Call to mind coworkers, neighbors, or family members of other faiths or no faith. What are you discovering about one another?

Instead, we can begin with a shared spiritual practice, like mindfulness, as a practical doorway for connection and understanding. We can practice mindfulness together with neighbors of other religions and no religion in order to open space to simply *be* in the present moment together, receptive to how God may show up. This is a different interfaith encounter than one that is about debate, comparing religious claims or critiquing ethical codes.

Of course, sharing in mindfulness practice requires thoughtful conversation and awareness of real differences. Mindfulness practice is shared but not identical across different religious and nonreligious traditions. As we recognize similarities, we must be careful to also recognize crucial differences and distinctives. We do not honor one another when we collapse or reduce all mindfulness practices into one, homogenous phenomenon. Thus, for example, while attentive breathing may involve similar steps for Christians and Buddhists, our understandings of what is happening in the experience and of its purpose will be different. Recognizing and honoring these differences is important in any interfaith encounter.

Warning: Mindfulness Disrupts

Assuredly, the practice of Christian mindfulness can bring greater awareness of God's presence, peace, and clarity. And that can turn life upside down! Like all spiritual practices, prayerful attentiveness is likely to disrupt the status quo. Life will not be the same.

As we become more present to our actual experience, we may be distressed by what we discover. For example, we may discover resentments that we harbor against our bosses or spouses. We may discover longings to change career paths or embark on new ministries that require risk-taking. We may be shocked to discover how much our egos are invested in a frenetic, busy schedule. We may find we cling to the honor badges of productivity and exhaustion. We may discover that the stories we tell ourselves about our lives just aren't true.

Moreover, as we strip away the cluttered surface of our lives, we may be disturbed by what we can now see in the open vista, especially the suffering of "the least of these." We are no longer numb to the cries of those hurting. We ache for the violence humans do to one another and to the earth. We see all people and all creation held within God's love and life. Our comfortable lives are disrupted as we ask new, hard questions.

Christian mindfulness appears deceptively simple, yet is life and world changing. The New Testament word for this kind of intentional, disruptive change is *metanoia*, a waking up and turning from the mindless path we have been stumbling on to the mindful path of abundant life in Christ. Jesus himself ties *metanoia* to the recognition that the reign of God is right here, right now when he says, "*Metanoeo* [Turn!]: Here comes the kingdom of heaven!" (Matt 4:17). Christian mindfulness of the present reign of God necessarily entails this change of heart and life. We might even call mindfulness a *converting* practice because it shakes us free from captivity to the world's ways and expectations so that we are converted (changed, turned) to God's ways and expectations. Such disruptive change helps us see the world more and more through God's eyes, increasing our love for neighbor and our commitment to justice and shalom for all.

This witness is so countercultural and against the runaway-train version of life that we must be prepared for misunderstanding or even rejection. Stopping to be present and pay attention in this moment can be judged as lazy, unproductive, or disengaged from Very Important Things. Reaching out to neighbors of other faiths through mindfulness practice may be labeled syncretism or going astray. Mindful social action might be criticized as too political or naive. Pushback will inevitably come when we challenge existing norms with Christian mindfulness. Perhaps mindfulness is one path to what Jesus means when he says, "All who want to save their lives will lose them. But all who lose their lives because of me will find them" (Matt 16:25). We must lose this surface life of cluttered distraction that the world calls productive in order to find our true lives for Jesus's sake.

Make no mistake: mindfulness practice will disrupt your life, changing you from the inside out. "Take your everyday, ordinary life—your sleeping, eating, going-to-work, and walking-around life—and place it before God....You'll be changed from the inside out" (Rom 12:1-2 The Message). Being "transformed by the renewing of your minds" so that we have "the attitude that was in Christ Jesus" can be wrenching, exhilarating, and life-changing in ways we cannot expect (Rom 12:2; Phil 2:5). It is always, *always*, the work of the Holy Spirit in us.

What do you fear may be disrupted about your life if you became more mindful of life with God? What do you hope will be disrupted?

But these discoveries both of ourselves and of the world, no matter how disruptive, are not the end of the story. Through Christian mindfulness, we also discover God's presence with us in the middle of our messy lives and messy world. We alone cannot heal our lives or heal the world, but, if mindful, we can participate in what God is doing and where God is leading.

Blessing the World

This book began with a description of our overstimulated culture in America and the sense of fragmentation and chronic distraction many experience as a result. One Christian spiritual practice to meet the hunger for real, rooted lives is mindfulness, a simple practice that has a long and rich tradition in Christian spirituality.

Our very lives can proclaim the reign of God at hand as we become more free, real, rooted, grateful, and compassionate to bless the world in Jesus's name through lives of justice and mercy.

Christian mindfulness is not the latest self-improvement gimmick or one more expression of the idolatry of American individualism. Any spiritual practice, Christian or otherwise, can become perverted by self-absorption. However, the proper *telos* of all Christian spiritual practices, including mindfulness, is not self-improvement. Rather, the proper end is to be transformed into Christlikeness, to participate in God's dream for the world. To be absolutely clear, if mindfulness practice stops at self alone then it fails as a Christian practice. On the other hand, this simple, accessible, adaptable spiritual practice can, through the Spirit's power, transform lives and bless the world.

That's why it's so important for Christian voices to join the wider conversation on mindfulness. Christian voices at the table can empower Christians in their daily lives to pay prayerful attention to God's abundant life and to live it. Pastors can help church members who already practice mindfulness at work or yoga class to understand its depth as a Christian spiritual practice, a way God is at work in their lives. Churchgoers looking to become less of a religious tourist and more of a spiritual pilgrim can explore Christian mindfulness to deepen their walk. The "spiritual but not religious" can discover a spiritual home in this Christian practice that anchors them in ancient wisdom and formative community.

We have examined the biblical roots of Christian mindfulness, showing both the distinctives and marks of a mindful Christian life (chapter 1). We identified some forms in Christian history (chapter 2), and offered applications for its practice today (chapter 3).

This last chapter articulates the disruptions and difference Christian mindfulness can make to bless the world God loves.

Time to get started, right here, right now. God the Holy Spirit will meet you where you are, in this present moment, inviting you into abundant life.

Group Study Guide

This Group Study Guide can be used in a six-week format or spread over more weeks as needed. Each week offers discussion questions and experiments for your group to try.

Week 1: Chapter 1

Discussion Questions

1. Read three of these Scripture passages out loud: Matthew 3:2; 4:17; 10:7; Mark 1:15; Luke 10:9; 10:11. What do you hear Jesus saying about the kingdom of God? How would you describe the kingdom of God?

2. How is the kingdom of God at hand in your life right now? Give examples.

3. Read Mark 4:9 and Matthew 13:16. In what ways do you have eyes to see and ears to hear? When you have "blessed eyes and ears," what happens?

4. Discuss the "Distinctives of Christian Mindfulness" in chapter 1. Do these ring true? What others would you add or change?

5. What marks of Christian mindfulness do you most long for in your life right now?

Experiments

1. Pay prayerful attention in discussion: Discuss the question, "How has God been portrayed to you? What is your primary image of God?" for about ten minutes. At the end of group discussion, observe thirty seconds of silence for each person to become aware of the sensations and feelings that arose in them during the discussion. Invite each person to share out loud one or two words that describe the sensations or feelings they have identified during the silence. Be careful not to fall into discussing the discussion. Rather, the focus here is on each person becoming mindful of himself or herself and God's presence here. Pause for more silence if that helps.

2. Review a news story from this week. When you consider it through "eyes to see and ears to hear the kingdom of God at hand," how does this affect your perception of the news story?

Week 2: Chapter 2

Discussion Questions

1. Discuss the notion that Christians are called to love the world without conforming to it. Do you agree or disagree? Why?

2. How do you curate the culture around you as a Christian? That is, how do you read cultural trends and values in daily life in order to make connections between your faith and the larger world? Discuss examples from your own life such as choosing which movie to watch or how to spend money.

3. Which, if any, of the Christian traditions in part 1 resonate with you? What other examples of mindfulness in Christian tradition come to mind?

4. Where in the larger culture have you encountered mindfulness practice, including health, business, education, or sports settings? What other examples of mindfulness in the culture come to mind?

5. What concerns or objections do you have about mindfulness as a Christian practice? What are you curious about or would you like to explore?

Experiments

1. Conduct an informal survey (either in person or by e-mail/social media) among your friends and family to find out who practices mindfulness and where they learned it. Bring survey results to group study to share and compare.

2. Conduct an informal survey (either in person or by e-mail/social media) within your church family to find out who practices mindfulness and where they learned it. You might survey folks at the next potluck, after worship, or at a committee meeting. Bring survey results to group study to share and compare.

Week 3: Chapter 3

Discussion Questions

1. Embodiment: Is your body a place you feel at home with God or Jesus? Why or why not?

2. Which practices or postures in chapter 3 speak to your desire for a more mindful Christian life? Notice the

differences and similarities among group members'
answers.

3. What other ways can you imagine incorporating Christian
mindfulness into your life right now?

Experiments

1. As a group, do the basic four-step method of Christian
mindfulness together. Read through it together first, then
ask one person to guide the group through the practice.

2. For next week: each person selects one practice or posture
from chapter 3 to try at home through the week. You
may want to journal your experience. At the next group
session, share your discoveries from this experience.

Week 4: More Practices

1. Discuss your experiences with the Christian mindfulness
practice you selected to experiment with through the last
week.

2. Select either the basic four-step method of Christian
mindfulness practice or another practice from chapter 3
to experiment with through the coming week. You may
want to journal the experience. Discuss your discoveries
at the next group meeting.

Week 5: Chapter 4

Discussion Questions

1. Think back to the marks of Christian mindfulness listed
in chapter 1. How do you need the good news of a freed,

real, rooted, grateful, and compassionate life right now? Who else do you know who is hungry for abundant life?

2. Do you agree or disagree that Christian mindfulness can make a difference in the world? Why?

3. What have you discovered about coworkers, neighbors, or family members of other faiths or no faith?

4. Discuss your experiences with the Christian mindfulness practice you selected to experiment with through the last week.

Experiments

1. Invite one other person—whether the person shares your faith, another faith, or no faith—to practice mindfulness with you for one day. You may choose to each practice it separately using your own method, or choose to meet to practice it together. Reflect on your experience and share your discoveries with the group. What did you learn about yourself, about God, or about mindfulness?

2. Interview a veteran practitioner of mindfulness about his or her experience. How has mindfulness disrupted or changed this person's life? How has it made a difference in the world? Or, invite the practitioner to your group for conversation.

3. Select either the basic four-step method of Christian mindfulness practice or another practice from chapter 3 to experiment with through the coming week. Discuss your experiences at the next group meeting.

Week 6: Wrap Up

Discussion Questions

1. What has clarified or changed about your understanding of mindfulness as a Christian practice?

2. What have you discovered about yourself, about God, about Christian spiritual life or about your group, through this study?

3. What are you now curious about or what do you want to explore further?

4. How might you incorporate Christian mindfulness into your existing spiritual practices?

Experiments

1. If this group meets regularly, commit to using the four-step basic Christian mindfulness practice to begin class meetings for the next six weeks. Designate one member to lead the group through the four steps, followed by spoken prayers of concern or thanksgiving. After six weeks, notice what happens and assess whether you want to continue.

2. Identify your current spiritual disciplines as individuals, as a class, and as a church. How might you incorporate Christian mindfulness into your existing spiritual practices? Make a plan to try a couple of your ideas.

Notes

1. Christian Mindfulness

1. Compare to the definition by leading proponent of mindfulness Jon Kabat-Zinn, "Mindfulness means paying attention in a particular way; On purpose, in the present moment, and nonjudgmentally." In *Wherever You Go, There You Are: Mindfulness Meditation in Everyday Life* (New York: Hyperion, 1994), 4.

2. This framework for prayer has been widely used, including Kathleen Norris, *The Cloister Walk* (New York: Riverhead, 1996); and Thomas Hart, *The Art of Christian Listening* (Mahwah, N.J.: Paulist, 1980).

3. See also Matthew 4:17; Luke 10:9-11.

4. For a thorough treatment of this motif in the New Testament, see Lövestam, *Spiritual Wakefulness in the New Testament*, trans. W. F. Salisbury. (Lund: Gleerup, 1963).

5. See similar stories in Luke 12:35-38; Mark 13:33-37.

6. See Romans 13:11; 1 Thessalonians 5:6; 1 Corinthians 16:13; Acts 20:31; Ephesians 6:18; and Colossians 4:2.

2. Curating Mindfulness in Christian Tradition and Contemporary Culture

1. See John 15:19; 17:14-19.

2. For discussion of missional life of the church, see Darrell Guder,

Missional Church: A Vision for the Sending of the Church in North America (Grand Rapids: Eerdmans, 1998); Alan J. Roxburgh and M. Scott Boren, *Introducing the Missional Church: What It Is, Why It Matters, How to Become One* (Grand Rapids: Baker, 2009); Christopher J. H. Wright, *The Mission of God: Unlocking the Bible's Grand Narrative* (Downers Grove, Ill.: InterVarsity, 2006).

3. Alice Robb, "How 2014 Became the Year of Mindfulness," *The New Republic*, December 31, 2014; Jeff Wilson, *Mindful America: The Mutual Transformation of Buddhist Meditation and American Culture* (New York: Oxford University Press, 2014); "The Mindful Revolution," *Time*, February 2014; Carolyn Gregoire and Joy Resmovitz, "How Mindfulness Has Changed the Way Americans Learn and Work," *Huffington Post*, May 22, 2015; David Gelles, *Mindful Work: How Meditation Is Changing Business from the Inside Out* (Boston: Houghton Mifflin Harcourt, 2015).

4. For a thorough treatment of spiritual battles in the writings of desert Christians, see Roberta C. Bondi, *To Pray and to Love: Conversation on Prayer with the Early Church* (Minneapolis: Augsburg Fortress, 1991). See also *Give Me a Word: The Alphabetical Sayings of the Desert Fathers*, Popular Patristics Series 52, ed. John Behr, trans. John Wortley (Yonkers, N.Y.: St Vladimir's Seminary Press, 2014); *The Sayings of the Desert Fathers*, trans. Benedicta Ward (Kalamazoo, Mich.: Cistercian, 1975, rev. 1984).

5. Evagrius Ponticus, *The Praktikos and Chapters on Prayer* (Kalamazoo, Mich.: Cistercian, 1972); John Cassian, *Conferences*, Classics of Western Spirituality (Mahwah, N.J.: Paulist, 1985).

6. The use of *apatheia* to mean "free of attachments or agendas" is not to be confused with common English use of "apathy," meaning "disinterest or lack of concern."

7. *The Sayings of the Desert Fathers*, 139.

8. St. Gregory of Sinai, *Philokalia*, ed. G. E. H. Palmer, P. Sherrard, and K. Ware (trans) (London: Faber & Faber, 1990), 4:212.

9. Jurgen Moltmann observes that the reason so much public prayer offered after 9/11 failed to draw people closer to God was "although we still associate religion with praying, we no longer associate praying with watching.... We no longer watchfully expect the coming God ahead of us.... The important thing is the watching." See Moltmann, "Watching for God," in *Walking with God in a Fragile World*, ed. James Langford and Leroy S. Rouner (Lanham, Md.: Rowman & Littlefield, 2002), 59.

10. *The Pilgrim's Tale*, ed. Aleksei Pentkovsky, trans. T. Allan Smith (Mahwah, N.J.: Paulist, 1999).

11. *Rb 1980: The Rule of St. Benedict*, trans. Timothy Fry (Collegeville, Minn.: Liturgical, 1981), 382.

12. *Devotio Moderna: Basic Writings*, ed. John H. Van Engen, Classics of Western Spirituality (Mahwah, N.J.: Paulist, 1988).

13. *Francis and Clare: The Complete Works*, trans. Regis J. Armstrong and Ignatius C. Brady, Classics of Western Spirituality (Mahwah, N.J.: Paulist, 1986).

14. William A. Barry, SJ, *Finding God in All Things: A Companion to the Spiritual Exercises of St. Ignatius* (Notre Dame, Ind.: Ave Maria, 2009), 3. See also *Ignatius of Loyola: The Spiritual Exercises and Selected Works*, ed. George E. Ganss, Classics of Western Spirituality (Mahwah, N.J.: Paulist, 1991).

15. Teresa of Jesus, *The Way of Perfection*, trans. E. Allison Peers (New York: Image Book/Doubleday, 1964).

16. "Spiritual Canticle," 1, 7–8, in *John of the Cross: Selected Writings*, trans. Kieran Kavanaugh, Classics of Western Spirituality (Mahwah, N.J.: Paulist, 1987).

17. Brother Lawrence, *The Practice of the Presence of God*, trans. John J. Delaney (New York: Image, 1977).

18. *Quaker Spirituality: Selected Writings*, ed. Douglas V. Steere, Classics of Western Spirituality (Mahwah, N.J.: Paulist, 1983).

19. Note also that "watching" sometimes referred to physically staying awake into the night to pray, as illustrated in the Watch Night Service. See also Amy Oden, "John Wesley's Notion of Watchfulness: 'A Mighty Exertion,'" *Wesleyan Theological Journal* 52 no. 1 Spring 2017.

20. Wesley included Brother Lawrence in his *Christian Library* of 1750–56. See *John and Charles Wesley, Selected Prayers, Hymns, Journal Notes, Sermon, Letters and Treatises*, ed. Frank Whaling, Classics of Western Spirituality (Mahwah, N.J.: Paulist, 1981), 10.

21. John Wesley, *Explanatory Notes upon the New Testament*, 3rd corrected ed. (Bristol: Graham and Pine, 1760–62), 2 Timothy 4:5.

22. John Wesley, "London Conference, May 1754," *Bicentennial Edition of the Works of John Wesley* (Nashville: Abingdon, 1984—), 10:283.

23. John Wesley, "Bristol Conference 1746," *Bicentennial Edition*, 10:182–83. Repeated in the Large Minutes of 1753–63, 10:902.

24. John Wesley, "MS Minutes: London Conference, June 1744," *Bicentennial Edition*, 10:133.

25. John Wesley, "Large Minutes of Several Conversations between the Rev Mr John and Charles Wesley and Others," *Bicentennial Edition*, 10:924.

26. E.g., Jon Kabat-Zinn, *Wherever You Go, There You Are: Mindfulness Meditation in Everyday Life* (New York: Hyperion, 1994; James Kingsland, *Siddhartha's Brain: Unlocking the Ancient Science of Enlightenment* (New York: William Morrow, 2016).

27. Zindel V. Segal, J. Mark G. Williams, John D. Teasdale, *Mindfulness-Based Cognitive Therapy for Depression: A New Approach to Preventing Relapse* (New York: Guilford, 2002); Matthew McKay, Jeffrey C. Wood, and Jeffrey Brantley, *The Dialectical Behavior Therapy Skills Workbook: Practical DBT Exercises for Learning Mindfulness, Interpersonal Effectiveness, Emotional Regulation and Distress Tolerance* (Oakland: New Harbinger, 2007); Sarah Bowen, Neha Chawla, and

G. Alan Marlatt, *Mindfulness-Based Relapse Prevention for Addictive Behaviors: A Clinician's Guide* (New York: Guilford, 2010). Russ Harris, *ACT Made Simple: An Easy-To-Read Primer on Acceptance and Commitment Therapy* (Oakland: New Harbinger, 2009); Nirbhay N. Singh, Giulio E. Lancioni, Subhashni D. Singh Joy, Alan S. W. Winton, Mohamed Sabaawi, Robert G. Wahler, and Judy Singh, "Adolescents with Conduct Disorder Can Be Mindful of Their Aggressive Behavior," *Journal of Emotional and Behavioral Disorders* 15, no. 1 (Spring 2007): 56–63; U.S. Department of Veterans Affairs (2011), "Mindfulness Practice in the Treatment of Traumatic Stress," http://www.ptsd.va.gov /public/pages/mindful-ptsd.asp.

28. National Health Service, "Mindfulness," http://www.nhs.uk /conditions/stress-anxiety-depression/pages/mindfulness.aspx; accessed March 22, 2016.

29. Yi-Yuan Tang, Yinghua Ma, Junhong Wang, Yaxin Fan, Shigang Feng, Qilin Lu, Qingbao Yu, Danni Sui, Mary K. Rothbart, Ming Fan, and Michael I. Posner, "Short-Term Meditation Training Improves Attention and Self-Regulation," *Proceedings of the National Academy of Sciences USA* 104, no. 43 (October 23, 2007): 17152–56; A. Lutz, . Brefczynski-Lewis, T. Johnstone, R. J. Davidson, "Regulation of the Neural Circuitry of Emotion by Compassion Meditation: Effects of Meditative Expertise," PLoS ONE 3, no. 3 (2007): 1; Christiane Wolf and J. Greg Serpa, *A Clinician's Guide to Teaching Mindfulness: The Comprehensive Session-by-Session Program for Mental Health Professionals and Health Care Providers* (Oakland: New Harbinger, 2015); F. Zeidan, J. A. Grant, C. A. Brown, J. G. McHaffie, and R. C. Coghill, "Mindfulness Meditation-Related Pain Relief: Evidence for Unique Brain Mechanisms in the Regulation of Pain," *Neuroscience Letters* 520, no. 2 (June 29, 2012): 165–73.

30. National Health Service, "Mindfulness as Good as Drugs for Preventing Depression Relapse," http://www.nhs.uk/news/2015/04April /Pages/Mindfulness-as-good-as-drugs-for-preventing-depression -relapse.aspx; accessed March 22, 2016.

31. Sara W. Lazar, Catherine E. Kerr, Rachel H. Wasserman, Jeremy

R. Gray, Douglas N. Greve, Michael T. Treadway, Metta McGarvey, Brian T. Quinn, Jeffery A. Dusek, Herbert Benson, Scott L. Rauch, Christopher I. Moore, and Bruce Fischi, "Meditation Experience Is Associated with Increased Cortical Thickness," *Neuroreport* 16, no. 17 (November 28, 2005): 1893–97.

32. A. A. Taren, J. D. Creswell, and P. J. Gianaros, "Dispositional Mindfulness Co-Varies with Smaller Amygdala and Caudate Volumes in Community Adults," *PLoS ONE* 8, no. 5 (2013).

33. Daniel D. Amen, *Change Your Brain, Change Your Life* (New York: Crown, 1998, 2015); Tom Ireland, "What Does Mindfulness Meditation Do to Your Brain?" *Scientific American,* June 12, 2014; Daniel J. Siegel, *The Mindful Brain: Reflection and Attunement in the Cultivation of Well-being* (New York: Norton, 2007; Jo Marchant, *Cure: A Journey into the Science of Mind over Body* (New York: Crown, 2016) and "Habits and Architecture," chapter 11 in Adam Alter, *Irresistible: The Rise of Addictive Technology and the Business of Keeping Us Hooked* (New York: Penguin Press, 2017).

34. Christina Congleton, Britta K. Holzel, and Sara W. Lazar, "Mindfulness Can Literally Change Your Brain," *Harvard Business Review,* January 8, 2015.

35. S. Baijal, A. P. Jha, A. Kiyonaga, R. Singh, and N. Srinivasan, "The Influence of Concentrative Meditation Training on the Development of Attention Networks during Early Adolescence," *Frontiers in Psychology* 2 (July 12, 2011), 1–9; M. Napoli, P. R. Krech, and L. C. Holley, "Mindfulness Training for Elementary School Students," *Journal of Applied School Psychology* 21, no. 1 (2005): 99–125; K. A. Schonert-Reichl, E. Oberle, M. S. Lawlor, D. Abbott, K. Thomson, T. F. Oberlander, and A. Diamond, "Enhancing Cognitive and Social-Emotional Development through a Simple-to-Administer Mindfulness-Based School Program for Elementary School Children: A Randomized Controlled Trial," *Developmental Psychology* 51, no. 1 (2005): 52–66; V. A. Barnes, L. B. Bauza, and F. A. Treiber, "Impact of Stress Reduction on Negative School Behavior in Adolescents," *Health and Quality of Life Outcomes* 10, no. 1 (2005): 1–7.

36. Kimberly A. Schonert-Reichl, et al, "Enhancing Cognitive and Social-Emotional Development through a Simple-to-Administer Mindfulness-Based School Program for Elementary School Children," 52–66.

37. Other resources include The Association for Mindfulness in Education (http://www.mindfuleducation.org), Mindful Life Project (http://mindfullifeproject.org), and Learning2Breathe Project at Johns Hopkins (http://learning2breathe.org).

38. Daniel Rechtschaffen, *The Way of Mindful Education: Cultivating Well-Being in Teachers and Students* (New York: Norton, 2014).

39. Joe Keohane, "In Praise of Meaningless Work: Mindfulness Mantras Are the Latest Tool of Corporate Control," *The Guardian*, April 7, 2015; David Brendal, "There Are Risks to Mindfulness at Work," *Harvard Business Review*, February 11, 2015.

40. Rachel W. Thompson, Keith A. Kaufman, Lilian A. De Petrillo, Carol R. Glass, and Diane B. Arnkoff, "One Year Follow-Up of Mindful Sport Performance Enhancement (MSPE) with Archers, Golfers, and Runners," *Journal of Clinical Sport Psychology* 5 (2011): 99–116; F. Gardner and Z. Moore, "A Mindfulness-Acceptance-Commitment-Based Approach to Athletic Performance Enhancement: Theoretical Considerations," *Behavior Therapy* 35, no. 4 (Autumn 2004): 707–23; Daniel Birrer, Philipp Röthlin, Gareth Morgan, "Mindfulness to Enhance Athletic Performance: Theoretical Considerations and Possible Impact Mechanisms," *Federal Institute of Sport*, Switzerland, May 2012; Timothy R. Pineau, Carol R. Glass, and Keith A. Kaufman, "Mindfulness in Sport Performance," *Handbook of Mindfulness*, ed. A. Ie, C. Ngnoumen, and E. Langer. Oxford: Wiley-Blackwell, 2014.

41. Lori Haase, April C. May, Maryam Falahpour, Sara Isakovic, Alan N. Simmons, Steven D. Hickman, Thomas T. Liu, and Martin P. Paulus, "A Pilot Study Investigating Changes in Neural Processing after Mindfulness Training in Elite Athletes," *Frontiers in Behavioral Neuroscience* (August 27, 2015): 9:229.

42. mPEAK, the Mindful Performance Enhancement, Awareness and Knowledge Mindfulness program, Center for Mindfulness at University of California, San Diego http://health.ucsd.edu/specialties /mindfulness/programs/mpeak/Pages/default.aspx; accessed March 12, 2016.

43. Kino MacGregor, "Discover the Power of the Present Moment in Yoga," *Psychology Today*, June 22, 2015; Nora Isaacs, "Practice Mindfulness in Yoga Poses," *Yoga Journal*, October 21, 2008.

44. C. L. Park, K. E. Riley, E. Bedesin, and V. M. Stewart, "Why Practice Yoga? Practitioners' Motivations for Adopting and Maintaining Yoga Practice," *Journal of Health Psychology* (July 16, 2014): 887–96.

45. Ibid.

46. Keohane, "In Praise of Meaningless Work"; Brendal, "There Are Risks to Mindfulness at Work"; Melanie McDonagh, "The Cult of 'Mindfulness,'" *The Spectator*, November 1, 2014.

47. Gelles, *Mindful Work*, 200–202.

48. Q13 Fox TV, "Parent Upset Children Taught 'Mindfulness' at School Yoga, Demand Changes, " Kennesaw, Ga., May 23, 2016, http://q13fox.com/2016/03/23/parent-upset-children-taught -mindfulness-at-school-yoga-demand-changes/.

3. Practices and Postures of Christian Mindfulness

1. Many instructions throughout this chapter refer to the four steps of the basic Christian mindfulness practice. For examples, see "Practicing the Presence of God," p. 57 and "Prayer of St. Patrick, p. 60. To review these basic building blocks, refer to pages 49–52 as needed.

2. "Patrick's Breastplate," in *Celtic Spirituality*, trans. Oliver Davies, Classics of Western Spirituality (Mahwah, N.J.: Paulist, 1999), 120.

3. Adapted from Daniel Wolpert, *Creating a Life with God: The Call of Ancient Prayer Practices* (Nashville: Upper Room, 2003), 180.

4. See discussion in chapter 2.

5. Teresa of Avila, *The Way of Perfection*, trans. E. Allison Peers (New York: Image Book/Doubleday, 1964), 28.

6. John Wesley, "Bristol Conference 1746," *The Bicentennial Edition of the Works of John Wesley* (Nashville: Abingdon, 1976–), 10:182–83. Repeated in the "Large Minutes of 1753–63," *Bicentennial Edition* 10:902.

7. Martin Luther King Jr., "the arc of the moral universe is long but it bends toward justice." The first instance of this phrase in King's work appears to be "Out of the Long Night," in *The Gospel Messenger*, Official Organ of the Church of the Brethren, Elgin, Illinois, February 8, 1958.

4. Christian Mindfulness Today

1. Adam Alter, *Irresistible: The Rise of Addictive Technology and the Business of Keeping Us Hooked* (New York: Penguin, 2017).

Printed in the USA
CPSIA information can be obtained
at www.ICGtesting.com
JSHW032255271023
50974JS00008B/218

9 781501 832499